Leaders Who Transform Society

Leaders Who Transform Society

What Drives Them and Why We Are Attracted

MICHA POPPER

Westport, Connecticut
London

Library of Congress Cataloging-in-Publication data

Popper, Micha, 1947–
    Leaders who transform society : what drives them and why we are attracted / Micha Popper.
        p. cm.
    Includes bibliographical references and index.
    ISBN 0-275-98561-X (alk. paper)
    1. Leadership.   2. Charisma (Personality trait)   I. Title.
    BF637.L4P653   2005
    158'.4–dc22   2005018645

British Library Cataloguing in Publication Data is available.

Library of Congress Catalog Card Number: 2005018645
ISBN: 0-275-98561-X

First published in 2005

Praeger Publishers, 88 Post Road West, Westport, CT 06881
An imprint of Greenwood Publishing Group, Inc.
www.praeger.com

Printed in the United States of America

The paper used in this book complies with the
Permanent Paper Standard issued by the National
Information Standards Organization (Z39.48-1984).

10 9 8 7 6 5 4 3 2 1

In memory of my mother, Livi Popper,
A woman who went through the holocaust,
yet did not believe in evil

Contents

Acknowledgments

Many people contribute to the writing of any book. There are colleagues and friends who help directly with advice and ideas or with feedback on a first draft. Sometimes an apt remark by a student in class or a chance conversation in the cafeteria sheds new light on a certain issue. In all these senses, many have contributed to this book. I am truly grateful to all of them and will thank them in person. However, sometimes there are people whose contribution is simply crucial, and this I wish to express here in writing. I want to thank Hazel Arieli, who has worked with me for more than ten years as translator and editor of all my books and of a large part of my ongoing academic work. Hazel is not simply a gifted translator and editor; she is an inexhaustible source of knowledge and ideas. There are aspects of my work that may never have seen the light of day without her curiosity, alertness, and broad erudition. But I owe gratitude to Hazel not only for her professional skills, but also for her qualities as a person: her responsibility, meticulousness, total reliability, and above all, caring and involvement in the best sense of true friendship. For all this, thank you, Hazel.

Chapter 1

ঙৣৡৣৡৣঙ

Introduction: What is Leadership?

"Man is only great when he acts from the passions."
Benjamin Disraeli

For many years now I have been teaching a university course called "the psychology of leadership." I usually commence the course by asking the students to mention some names of people whom they perceive as leaders. This little "experiment" (which I have repeated with various groups of people who differed in age, sex, and education) quickly yields a list of well-known names, many of which appear in nearly all the groups, names such as John Kennedy, David Ben Gurion, Moses, Jesus, Charles de Gaulle, Hitler, Mahatma Gandhi, Martin Luther King, Nelson Mandela, Mussolini, Yitzhak Rabin, Jeanne d'Arc, Theodore Herzl, Churchill, Franklin Delano Roosevelt, Lee Kuan Yew, Moshe Dayan, Abraham Lincoln, Mao Tse-tung, Ataturk, George Washington, Anwar Sadat, and Margaret Thatcher. After writing the names on the board, I ask the group to examine the list and seek some kind of governing order in an attempt to formulate a possible model that can cast light on leadership as a **phenomenon**. "In fact," I say to them, "this list is a personification of a social psychological phenomenon, and the question you were asked was designed to concretize a phenomenon that is perhaps too abstract for discussion." It soon emerges that it is hard to characterize a leadership model that has a reasonable degree of generalization. The list of leaders includes tall people (Abraham Lincoln) and short people (David Ben Gurion); excellent orators (Martin Luther King) and some who were notoriously poor speakers (Moses, who is described in the Bible as "slow of speech," or Yitzhak Rabin); handsome people (Kennedy) as well as some who were clearly unprepossessing; people with almost prophetic vision (Theodore Herzl) alongside pragmatic ones (Franklin Roosevelt); some who set a personal example in their daily behavior (Gandhi), and others whose hedonistic behavior made them the subject of controversy (Moshe Dayan); people whose personal influence encouraged tolerance and reduced violence (Gandhi, Mandela), and others whose influence inflamed evil impulses and wreaked destruction and devastation (Hitler, Mussolini). Moreover, some of those on the list were perceived by a certain society as extremely charismatic leaders in one period, but not in another period; sometimes this was the case even within a short time span (Winston Churchill, Moshe Dayan). Some figures are perceived as the embodiment of leadership in one place, but not in another. To sum up, the conclusions that emerge from this discussion match the argument of James MacGregor Burns, writer of one of the most frequently quoted books on leadership, that "Leadership is the most observed and least understood phenomenon on earth."[1] I believe it was this conclusion, that leadership is a multifaceted and elusive phenomenon given to diverse definitions that underlies the psychological research on leadership. The fact is that the thousands of studies collected in handbooks on leadership[2] always describe very specific aspects of leadership. Some of them attempt to identify and describe typical consistent behaviors of leaders, particularly of outstanding leaders or those considered successful.[3] Some of the studies focus on the leader's functioning as a decision maker,[4] as expressed with some degree of exaggeration by a writer on political leadership in the United States: "We don't pay the President of the US to work hard, at the end of the day we pay him for (one, two . . . four) major decisions that he makes during his term of office."[5] Some studies discuss leadership in terms of cognitive models that deal with information processing, which attempt to identify patterns and find some order in followers' perceptions of leaders.[6] There are some scholars who treat leadership as a psychodynamic phenomenon, often comparing the leader to a parent (usually a father) who is supposed to fulfill psychological parental functions, which are mainly that of providing a sense of security.[7] Scholars with a more sociological orientation do not ascribe great weight to the leader's internal psychological processes. In their view, it is more important to understand the representative value of the leader[8] as a symbol of processes, social forces, or simply as an expression of longing for change in the social order.[9] One way or another, leadership is discussed and studied from the specific angle of a particular discipline or by the observation and examination of clearly defined and, above all, measurable cognitive or behavioral variables. For many years this was also my approach to the subject, both in teaching and in research. In teaching, I simply divided leadership into separate "departments" as presented in the research literature,[10] and in research, like the others in the field, I investigated certain specific angles that interested me personally. However, in the course of my intensive occupation with the leadership phenomenon, I became more strongly aware of what was present and what was absent in the discussion on leadership. For example, the repetitive use of similar arguments differently worded, the emphasis in the research on statistically measurable variables, the emphasis placed on the generalizability of statistical data, while ignoring attempts to interpret and understand in depth the processes that underlie the overt behaviors or attitudes of both leaders and followers. But what mainly disturbed me was the absence of a more overall approach or conceptual framework permitting analysis of leadership in a more fundamentally psychological, more comparative view, like the approaches that have developed in certain areas of psychology, particularly in social psychology.[11]

And thus, my uncomfortable feeling of "holes in the discussion" gradually grew, and with it grew new thoughts, focusing first on the attempt to understand better the conceptual difficulty in creating a more integrative discussion. Later, alternative ideas arose, and I began jotting down thoughts and ideas on the subject with increasing rapidity and intensity over the years. It is hard to describe to most readers the conditions for incubation of ideas furnished by academic life. My variegated career, which has included management, command, consultation, and in the past decade academic teaching and research, enables me to see this more clearly. Generally, people engaged in academic frameworks probe into the subjects they deal with to a depth unparalleled in other frameworks (this, perhaps, is the major contribution of academic organizations). Thus, the notes jotted down on my desk, in cafes, on trains, airplanes, at conventions, during discussions with students, at traffic lights and even in the intermission during movies, coalesced into this attempt, which first materialized in my teaching and supervision of student's theses and later crystallized into this book. The underlying aim of this endeavor was not simply to offer another addition of knowledge in a specific field of leadership research; many books and papers have done that. My thoughts evolved into an impulse that became stronger and stronger as I felt a more integrative perception crystallizing in me. When I had a powerful feeling (based on years of observation, study, and thought) that I could do it, my urge to write the book became irrepressible. I hope I am not deluding or deceiving either myself or others with this feeling.

It seems to me that the difficulty in developing discussion, and certainly research, on leadership in the directions I have indicated lies in the fact that leadership, particularly the type described as "charismatic," is above all an emotional phenomenon. This argument, although it matches my personal experience, is not merely intuitive.[12] Zajonc,[13] in a prize-winning article entitled "Feeling and thinking: Preferences need no inferences," summarizes many studies on the classic debate between cognition and emotion; he argues simply: "People do not risk their lives for freedom because of a precise cognitive analysis of the pros and cons" (p. 172) and they certainly do not do so in matters of preference. Preference is a matter of emotions (and the explanations and assessments come later). This is revealed in almost every meeting with people we don't know, including, almost ironically, business meetings, which are supposed to be "purely cognitive and rational." (Words such as "chemistry" or "click" are often used to express this situation). Charismatic leaders are also a matter of emotional preference, as many studies have shown. For example, researchers found that leaders graded as more charismatic were those who simply aroused more emotions.[14] One illustration of this is the charismatic leaders' more frequent use of images that have an emotional effect. Martin Luther King did not say "I have an idea," but "I have a dream," which is a much more emotional image. Churchill, in his important speeches, used images that appealed to the emotions ("blood, sweat, and tears") rather than pure facts. The interesting point is that the emotional effect is not only part of the phenomenon itself, but also part of the observation and discussion of the phenomenon. For example, for most Americans, "leadership" arouses positive emotions. "To be a leader" is a desirable characteristic, worthy of aspiration. Moreover, successes, certainly successes in organizations, are usually attributed to the leader of the organization. The popularity of books on leaders of organizations, such as Jack Welch of GE or Lee Iacocca of Chrysler, demonstrates this clearly.[15] However, the Japanese, for example, are revolted by the mystification of leaders and never attribute organizational successes to a specific leader.[16] Among the French there is a considerable degree of doubt and fear of charismatic leaders. Serge Moscovici pointed out: "When they speak to us of a leader, we think, like in conditioning, like a reflex, of Hitler. . . . Because of history, everything we see that points to leadership seems to us to be the unwelcome result of distortions of democracy."[17] However, as stated, the main difficulty lies in interpreting the emotions that are involved in the leadership phenomenon. Here is an example from the field of leadership in organizations that was presented in a comparative study of Japanese and Americans.[18] A manager – a leader in an organization – who asks an employee why he has been absent from work will be regarded by the Japanese worker as taking an interest in his welfare and, therefore, as a considerate and sensitive leader. The very same behavior might be regarded by an American worker as invasive, as a gross violation of human rights. Furthermore, leadership exists in diverse contexts: in the military, in industry, in communities, and in various social groups. Clearly, these systems differ in many aspects, including the dimensions of leadership. Nevertheless, as we saw from the "experiment" mentioned at the beginning of this chapter, most people draw their images of leaders and leadership, as well as their own intuitive theories of leadership, from exposure to images of political leaders. This applies not only to "amateurs," but also can be seen among scholars who are regarded as experts. The wave of psychological studies that emerged after the publication of James MacGregor Burns' book, *Leadership*, illustrates this argument. Burns, a political historian, writes about political leaders and discusses mainly American leaders, such as Theodore and Franklin Roosevelt, Woodrow Wilson, and John Kennedy. To Burns, leadership in its true and important sense is first and foremost an influence on conceptual dimensions that is manifested in more moral behavior on the part of the followers. When Burns' ideas were translated into models and measures for the purpose of research on leadership in organizations,[19] the motivational aspect, which is related to results, became the focus of examination and discussion, whereas the moral aspect shrank in importance and was almost ignored.[20] Thus, although scholars who study leadership in organizations use exactly the same terms proposed by Burns, the contents and the emphases are different. There is obviously different emphasis on the research variables when investigating leadership outside the political sphere. Moreover, there is often a degree of romanticization in the description of political leaders,[21] who are usually described in terms of **traits**, which are sometimes exalted ones.[22] On the other hand, scholars observing and studying leaders in organizations, communities, or social groups, although they often use the same concepts, tend to formulate them in terms of specific behaviors.[23] Much has been said of **leadership behaviors**, some of which are classified as "charismatic behaviors."[24] Thus, because leadership is a phenomenon that exists in almost every social context, the variety of perspectives and units of analysis blurs the essence, the core of the phenomenon. What does the leader of a political party have in common with the spiritual leader of a religious congregation? Is the influence of national leaders composed of the same "materials" as that of outstanding leaders in business organizations or distinguished military commanders? Or are the differences between these cases too big to allow for a general theory or even for general assumptions on leadership? The argument that will be expanded in the book is that despite differences in circles of influence, number of followers and their characteristics, types of mission, degree of proximity or distance from the leader – all of which are undoubtedly bound up with various expectations, dynamics, and criteria of success and failure – there is a basic rule present in all the manifestations of leadership, and if we look at leadership from the viewpoint suggested here, this rule will enable us to see both the similarities and differences in the various manifestations of leadership existing in different contexts. The viewpoint proposed is the conceptualization of leadership as **relationship**. This viewpoint allows us to see the unique aspects of individual leaders and of different types of leadership, such as political leadership, military leadership, leadership in industry or in social movements, but does not prevent us from seeing the broad context. In other words, the framework suggested permits us to see both the picture and the background.

Metaphorically, this can be likened to an action shot as opposed to a still photograph, which freezes a situation at a given moment (the quantitative approach that is prevalent in research). The conceptualization of leadership as relationship allows us to see not only the action itself, but also the movements in the background and the circumstances in which the relationship exists (and changes). It permits analysis of specific cases of leadership along with integrative-comparative analysis.

The general argument is as follows: wherever there is leadership, there is a leader and there are followers. The political leader has supporters and voters, the military leader has subordinates, the leader in industry has workers, the spiritual leader has believers, and so forth. In all these cases, the informal relations existing between the leader and the followers will affect their willingness to act, especially in a space that is above and beyond the instructions and the practices of work by the book.[25] I saw a simple and unmistakable test of this in the responses of workers to two managers' requests to work during the weekend on an urgent project. The workers of one of the managers said, "They can't force us to do it [according to their work contracts], and we are not prepared to undertake this effort. We have families and other commitments," whereas the workers of the other manager in the same plant, working in the same conditions, said, "Although we don't have to, we always respond to our manager's requests and make every effort to help him." Simply put, the second manager has more "leadership quality." The deeper meaning of this expression is that the second manager's relationship with his workers is of a different emotional quality from that of the first, and this gives him greater influence over them. This applies to every leadership situation. There is always a relationship; sometimes based on a purely instrumental dynamic of give and take (promotion, interest, reward for effort), as is common in business organizations. But sometimes, and these are the more "classic" cases, the relationship is based on a more complex emotional attachment. The attachment of a believer to his spiritual leader, or of an ardent supporter to a political leader, or a soldier's willingness to follow his commander into battle – these include complex emotional layers that are not necessarily always on the conscious level, but it is the emotional relationship that gives rise to the more outstanding expression of leadership.

I wish to argue that the relationship between leaders and their followers is based on **need** – a concept that has been much discussed in psychological literature. My argument (which will be elucidated in Chapter 3) is that leader-follower relations are rooted in the needs of both sides. Out of the many theories dealing with needs, I have chosen two theoretical frameworks that are integrative and particularly relevant to the discussion at hand: Maslow's needs theory,[26] one of the most quoted theories in psychology, which served Burns in his monumental book on leadership[27] and Alderfer's needs theory,[28] which was greatly influenced by Maslow's theory and complements it in many aspects relevant to the present discussion. According to these theories, people need security, belonging, social identity, meaning, and development. In leader-follower relations, the needs of the followers are expressed in wishes, longing, perceptions, attributions, and projections. In general, certain needs come to the fore in different circumstances, and this is reflected in the changing wishes. For example, in situations of crisis and uncertainty (e.g., in wartime), the need for security becomes dominant and the longing for a "strong man" who radiates the ability to answer this need will be stronger than in everyday circumstances.[29] In the absence of a solid identity (during the establishment of a social movement or of a state), the individual who best symbolizes a clear and worthy social identity will be perceived as a leader.[30] People who are regarded as capable of a distinct contribution in the sphere of making and managing meaning or who transmit a sense of ideational, moral, or other development connected with the desired self image of the followers (e.g., spiritual leaders)[31] will be perceived as leaders as long as these desires are dominant. The formation of these dynamic patterns is marked by a certain regularity that will be discussed in this book.

I wish to emphasize that the distinction is not as clear and simple as it may sound. The relations with the leader may be based on several needs simultaneously, and some needs, according to theorists of psychodynamic schools, are not always on the conscious level. Moreover, it is not always a question of a relationship with a living being. Sometimes the followers maintain a relationship with a **representation** of an idea or a longing personified by a leader, even if he is not alive. For example, ten years after the death of the Lubavitcher Rabbi (the head of a worldwide movement of ultra-orthodox Jews – the Habad Hasidim), many of his followers still "receive" messages and even instructions from him. And also in the case of living leaders, the relations are, by definition, two-way, and the leaders have their own needs, which extend over a broad range, from the need for power,[32] which may be more intense among leaders than among others, through narcissistic needs, such as the need for admiration,[33] to the need to leave their stamp. This need may be manifested in many ways; the simplest and most common of them being the need to bring children into the world in order to ensure a form of continuity and perpetuation. Artists aspire to leave their stamp through their works.[34] Similarly, certain leaders are motivated by the need to leave their stamp, whether in concrete physical form (such as monuments) or in the hearts of their followers. It is not by chance that national leaders speak of their place and role in history, and leaders at other levels, such as social or community leaders, talk about imprinting a vision or similar phrases expressing the wish to make a mark that will last beyond their physical presence.

Leadership is also in some senses a form of parenthood – a need that exists in most people,[35] but which may assume a more generalized expression among leaders. At all events, leader-follower relations in most cases (except for the link to dead leaders, which will be discussed later) are the outcome of the meeting between the needs and desires of the leader and those of the followers. When there is harmony between these needs, leadership relations will develop. As stated, this meeting occurs according to a certain order that can be interpreted through understanding of the three components: the followers' needs, the leader's needs, and the circumstances of the encounter. It is important to note that this is not a static situation; the needs change, both because the circumstances change and because of the dynamic nature of all relationships (e.g., romantic love or friendship).

This is the general framework of the substructure that generates **dynamic patterns** of needs and desires. In Chapter 3, I will present illustrations and explanations of the most salient dynamic patterns, which may be seen as prototypes of leadership relations, and within this general perspective I will focus on the type of relationship known in the literature as transformational leadership. This is the kind of leadership that generates changes in the followers' moral values and development. The rationale and the structure of the book are as follows: The second chapter is a bird's-eye view of leadership, which is aimed at reviewing briefly how leadership was conceptualized and studied throughout the years. The purpose of this overview is to provide the background for better understanding of the attempt at innovation in the discussion that appears in the ensuing chapters.

Chapter 3 is a critical discussion of the main perspectives on leadership. After a review and analysis of biases existing in leadership research, I will expand the discussion on leadership as relationship, focusing on three patterns of leader-follower relations: 1) regressive relations, 2) developmental relations, and 3) symbolic relations.

Chapter 4 deals with transformational leadership, which is a specific type of relationship between leaders and followers. The dynamics, the influence, and the concrete psychological effects of such relationships are demonstrated at the beginning of the chapter, citing outstanding cases. Each of the leaders referred to is a dominant representative of a particular aspect of transformational leadership. A few examples will illustrate this. Historians and political scientists found much to criticize in various aspects of the personality and leadership of Abraham Lincoln, Franklin Delano Roosevelt, Mahatma Gandhi, Theodore Herzl, and Nelson Mandela. However, it is generally agreed that after Lincoln's presidency the United States was not the same as before in terms of ethics and values; it had undergone a **transformation,** and the patterns of legitimization and the criteria of what is "right" and "wrong" had changed radically.[36] Franklin Delano Roosevelt was, in the opinion of some eminent historians, a figure lacking intellectual inspiration; some even thought him pragmatic to the point of superficiality.[37] Yet few question the view that America was lucky to have Roosevelt as president in such difficult periods as the Depression of the 1930s and World War II. They all agree that Roosevelt played a key role in the empowerment of millions of Americans, who sensed that they could draw strength from his composure, his self confidence, his amazing control, and felt that they could overcome all the difficulties and win the battle. For those Americans, Roosevelt was the man who helped them to discover their hidden strengths and make them a personal and collective force.[38]

Mahatma Gandhi, Theodore Herzl, and Nelson Mandela were figures with complex personalities,[39] who did not escape criticism, yet no one doubts that their leadership wrought a transformation in the sphere of motivation. Through their leadership they were able to recruit millions of oppressed people and imbue them with new energies.

The main idea is, therefore, that transformational leaders are those whose leadership creates in Burns' terms, a transformation. Just as an electric transformer changes the current, so a transformational leader changes feelings, patterns of thinking, and behavior. Such leaders cause their believers to be "much more" than they were before their meeting with the leader, to be more motivated, to believe more in their own strength, to be more ethical and social-minded in their thoughts and deeds. Although this claim is not new, the analyses existing in the literature do not go deeply into the profound psychological processes that create this powerful effect.[40] Chapter 4 attempts to do this, namely, not to focus on the "bottom line" of the leader's achievements or on the unfolding of events (which has been done by historians in a myriad of books and articles), but to analyze the psychological process that made these transformations possible. There is a pattern in this process, as will be shown. Furthermore, I argue that such leadership processes take place not only at the level of leaders of nations or vast organizations. The cases mentioned previously (which are described at length in the book) are outstanding ones that I use to demonstrate some of the key arguments on the assumption that the readers know these famous leaders and their actions. However, leadership of this kind, of this psychological quality, occurs in everyday life, too, such as in family units, schools, youth movements, factorys, military units, and, in fact, in every social organization that exists over time. Indeed, the second part of the chapter moves from the large historical figures to the description and analysis of transformational leadership in everyday life.

Chapter 5, "The development of transformational leaders," is largely innovative, both conceptually and empirically. Due to the lack of researchable theoretical concepts, the development of leaders has barely been investigated beyond the biographical paradigm, which has been dealt with extensively, mainly by historians. There have been some impressive attempts at psychological analysis of leaders, but the emphasis in those works is on psychoanalytic thinking (Erikson on Gandhi)[41] and there is also much stress on destructive leaders, such as Hitler (Burns).[42] The chapter engages in an attempt to understand the development of three elements:

1. Motivation to lead – why do certain people want to be leaders and is there some kind of order in patterns of motivation?
2. What comprises the psychological ability to be a leader?
3. What is that special ability that makes a leader a transformational leader, one who acts with a social orientation beyond purely narcissistic aims of self-aggrandizement?

   These questions, apart from being the major subject of my research, have scarcely been examined. The chapter presents some new arguments, as well as recent research results.

The concluding chapter, in addition to summarizing the argumentation presented in the book, also offers a broader perspective of observation.

It attempts to understand the phenomenon of transformational leadership beyond its psychological dynamic and to look at the meaning of the burgeoning rhetoric on transformational leadership. Is it a passing fashion? Or does this rhetoric signify part of a process that the German philosopher Friedrich Hegel called "the spirit of wisdom,"[43] that is to say, development toward a more enlightened world in which transformational leadership is part of the culture and not just a psychological phenomenon existing between a certain leader and his followers? Such a discussion also permits identification of clearer criteria of transformational leadership compared with other types of leadership.

Finally, a few personal words about the structure and style of this book: one of the major difficulties I experienced in writing the book concerned decisions as to the level of detail in the body of the book. For example, I was very much occupied with the question as to how much detail I should enter into when discussing various studies or theories and models. The extremes are almost always clear. At one extreme, in academic journals one writes according to accepted formats, describing in detail research variables and the procedure followed in conducting the research, whereas presenting a broad review of previous studies conducted in the same field. At the other extreme, in popular writing the opposite approach usually prevails, targeting as broad an audience as possible. Some of the dilemmas I faced resulted from my wish to write a book somewhere in between these two orientations. On the one hand, I did not want to write a book to be read only by students on the lecturer's recommendation (which is usually obligatory). On the other hand, I certainly wanted the arguments presented in the book to be backed up by previous knowledge accumulated in thousands of studies and observations by people whose work and thought on the subject can teach us a great deal. To avoid a confusing profusion of detail, the body of the text presents the arguments developed in the book, and the endnotes provide information on studies, models, and theories from which some of these arguments are derived. The decisions about what to "put in parentheses" were sometimes hard. In many cases I am not at all sure that these points should appear in the notes rather than in the body of the text. Therefore, I invite the reader to follow the notes in sequence. Although this kind of parallel reading is not always technically convenient, I believe it is worthwhile.

Chapter 2

❦

A Bird's-eye View of Leadership

In politics, in the work place, in the local community, the street gang, the military, in schools, youth movements, even in kindergartens, leadership is a phenomenon that can be identified and described and attributed to certain individuals whose influence is palpable, yet there is a large gap between the everyday observation of leadership in action and the ability to investigate it as an important social phenomenon. In referring to this gap, leadership scholars have used various images. For example, some compared leadership to romantic love. "Leadership is like love," claimed Charles Lindholm, that is, all people are busy with it but understand it very little.[1] Other scholars have described leadership through images that all point to the elusiveness of the phenomenon. "Like the Abominable Snowman in the legend," wrote one of the scholars, "you see his footprints everywhere but you don't see the man." And as in legends, words like "magic" or "charisma" (meaning a gift of God) appear in numerous titles of articles on leadership.[2]

Despite the "mysticism" of the phenomenon, there is no evidence of a decline in the desire to study and write about leadership in various disciplines (particularly history, political science, sociology, and psychology). This in itself indicates what a fascinating and important topic it is. In this chapter, I will present a bird's-eye view of the main trends in the discourse and research on leadership in the hope that such an overview will provide a clearer understanding of the attempt at innovation in the discussion that appears in the following chapters.

Looking beyond the different disciplines, we see that the literature dealing with leadership has approached it from three points of departure: one emphasized the leader, the second emphasized the circumstances of the emergence of leadership, and the third emphasized the followers as the source of mental creation of leaders. I will briefly review the gist of the arguments presented from each of these points of departure.

THE LEADER

The systematic discussion on leadership first appeared among the early philosophers. Plato, in his essays on the philosopher king, deals with the issue of who is capable and worthy of being a leader. Comparing leadership to sailing a ship, Plato states that neither physical strength nor popularity with the sailors will keep the ship safely afloat. The true captain, says Plato, is the one who must consider the seasons of the year and the time of day, the sky, the stars and the winds, and everything that belongs to that art, if he is really to be the man who is worthy of controlling the ship.[3] Plato focuses mainly on the question of who is worthy of being a leader. His answer: The one who knows. But this does not mean knowledge in the technical sense; knowledge, according to Plato's teachings, is knowledge of an IDEA, and the person who heads a state has to understand the IDEA of the state. And because knowledge of the IDEA of the state is rooted in broad moral, political and philosophical knowledge, the leader has to reach the highest level of knowledge. This argument has practical implications: if the leader is one who knows, and if knowledge means, among other things, knowledge of justice, and if the leader is one who fulfills this IDEA – then government cannot serve as a tool for the leader's personal gain. The position of leadership is designed to serve justice and the good of the majority. Leadership, to Plato, is more of a duty than a right; therefore, the leader has to be devoid of any private interest. For example, Plato requires leaders to lack all private property.

And where will the leaders come from? Plato developed a kind of class theory, in which society is divided according to the type of souls its members possess. For example, the greedy will compose the merchant class, whereas the philosopher kings are people who are endowed with the highest type of soul – the wise. The leader, then, is one who was endowed at birth with a soul that prepares him for his role. Nevertheless, he has to undergo a thorough education in all aspects of human knowledge in order to be worthy of his role. Indeed, Plato's theory already contained the question that has exercised modern scholars: are some people born leaders or do they become leaders by virtue of circumstances, training, and development?

A similar view of the leader as a "great man" was presented by the nineteenth-century philosopher, Thomas Carlyle, who referred to the leader as "hero" in his famous treatise "On heroes and the work of heroes." However, unlike Plato's thought, Carlyle sees the leader as worthy not because of his knowledge of the IDEA but because of his exceptional talents. Although Plato and Carlyle differ in their views of the sources of leadership, both of them see the leader as a source of doing good, of contributing to society. Plato regards the leader as a personification of a moral idea, whereas Carlyle, who expresses the Romantic stream in philosophy, sees the leader as a paternalistic aristocrat who acts out of love, belief, and innocence to establish and maintain an ideal community.[4]

Niccolo Machiavelli ascribes to the leader exclusive influence in shaping reality. In this, he resembles Plato and Carlyle, but, unlike them, he does not see the leader as expressing a higher moral essence or even necessarily a wish to do good. According to Machiavelli, the name of the game is power and personal gain. Machiavelli's leader is not motivated by any ideal, but purely and simply by the lust for power. Hence, the idea does not dictate any rules of behavior but at most serves as a means of acquiring the benefits of power.[5]

The ideas that were discussed theoretically and abstractly by philosophers who took an interest in leadership are clearly reflected in the psychological research on leadership. The first empirical approach to the study of leadership was called the "great man" approach (or, as psychologists tended to call it, the "trait approach") and was based on the assumption (like Carlyle's) that the leader was a person endowed with exceptional qualities that gave him the power to influence people. The first research conducted according to this orientation was that of Terman in 1904.[6] In this study, Terman attempted to identify traits of student leaders through observation in the school as well as reports of teachers and students. The findings of this study testified to the convergence between leaders identified by the researcher as leaders and those identified as such by their schoolmates and teachers. The leaders' characteristics that were identified indicated that leaders are superior to their classmates in physical size, style of dress, courage, eloquence, external appearance, and reading habits.

A growing volume of studies of this kind in different variations and more complex research designs followed Terman's experiments. As early as 1948, Stogdill surveyed 124 leadership studies examining scores of traits that were thought to differentiate between leaders and non-leaders.[7] Some of the studies that followed Terman examined physical characteristics such as external appearance and height. Others examined characteristics such as intelligence, resoluteness, originality, and so forth. Many studies contradicted each other; for example, traits that were identified in one study did not appear in others. Altogether, in the 1950s, when this kind of research was conducted in large volume, it was not possible to make a clear and comprehensive statement about the observable and measurable characteristics of leaders or about the weight of these characteristics. It emerged that both philosophical thinking and the psychological thinking of scientific research were unable to explain leadership by relating solely to the leaders' characteristics. After this period, there was a decline in the trait approach for a period of thirty years, whereas new approaches emphasizing other variables were developed (these will be reviewed later).

Following the disappointment with the study of leaders' traits, a more modest approach, though still focused on the leaders, was adopted in psychological research – the study of leaders' **behaviors**. This change can be understood not only as a result of disappointment with the trait approach but also in connection with the development of general psychological research. During the 1940s and 1950s, those who set the tone in psychological research aspired to give psychology a scientific flavor, and because the sole form of science was the natural sciences, the mainstream psychological studies were based on observable and measurable variables. This approach was controversial, as it was viewed as being very technical and limited. However, the observation of behavior (in an expanded and updated version) had a new lease on life in the 1980s and gained momentum from conceptual and methodological developments contributed by scholars who were deeply influenced by the book *Leadership*, which was written by the political historian, James McGregor Burns. This book, which deals with leaders who wrought far-reaching moral changes in their followers,[8] had particular influence on Bernard Bass, one of the better-known psychologists in the United States, who examined leadership in organizations. Inspired by Burns's ideas, Bass conducted studies in a book that offered researchable conceptualizations and tools for measuring "leadership in everyday life."[9] This book also returned the leaders to center stage in psychological research, but, in contrast to the past, pointed to various combinations of behaviors that create differential leadership **styles**. In fact, leadership research today deals largely with the influence of different styles (mostly measured by questionnaires developed by Bass and his students) on dependent variables such as satisfaction, level of motivation, commitment, involvement, and followers' level of performance.

On the face of it, this is a return to the "great man" paradigm, but in fact it is a spiral return, and although it restores the centrality of the leader, its basic assumptions are different. What we see here is not Carlyle's assumption that leaders have "God-given" talents and qualities, nor Plato's assumption of the philosopher-king. Perhaps the reverse is true, leaders are like everybody else, but they **behave** in a way that has powerful influence on others. Their influence stems from the frequency of influential behaviors and, therefore, it is necessary to examine these behaviors without dealing with the leaders' personalities – this was the dominant paradigm in leadership research until the end of the 1990s.

During the 1990s, research in the psychology of leadership developed in new directions – directions that can also be discerned in the writings of philosophers. For example, the tacit assumption of psychological research (especially American) was that leadership is a positive phenomenon. But history has seen leaders like Hitler, who were outstanding in the basic sense of leadership; they influenced and even swept up millions of people, although their leadership was blatantly immoral and even destructive. Psychological research, unlike disciplines such as philosophy, had tended for many years to avoid ethical issues, which were not seen as psychological issues because they were content-related rather than psychological processes.[10] However, in the 1990s psychological research began to deal with the distinction between positive and negative leaders. Machiavelli's speculations regarding the motives and sources of influence of leaders thus became 1990s topics of research in the psychology of leadership.[11]

The theoretical developments that appear to be most significant in the realm of psychological knowledge, particularly in the understanding of the "internal world" of the individual, occurred after the first third of the twentieth century. The monumental contributions of Sigmund Freud, Erik Erikson, Alfred Adler, Carl Gustav Jung, Melanie Klein, Heinz Kohut, Otto Kernberg, John Bowlby, and many others advanced the understanding of the development of internal representations that guide the individual's emotions and behaviors throughout his life. At the beginning of the twentieth century these contributions were mainly theoretical, partly because the study of emotions was still not considered scientific or researchable. But in the second half of the century – especially following approaches suggested by Bowlby, as well as conceptual and methodological developments in the study of emotions – part of this thinking became researchable, which led to the rapid development of empirical research in characterization of personality and its development from childhood to old age.[12]

Thus, since the heyday of the trait approach, a great deal of relevant new knowledge has been accumulated in general psychology, permitting scholars to return and examine the personality of the leader using concepts and tools that did not exist during the early days of leadership research. And in fact, we witness a renewal of research interest in leaders, but this time it is not a question of their "objective" characteristics or their behaviors, but of psychological personality aspects that are the source of their behaviors and manifestations of leadership. In other words, what we now see is the exploration of deeper and more dynamic levels than those proposed by the trait approach. Scholars returning to this angle of research can examine variables such as level of anxiety, self efficacy, locus of control, optimism, and similar psychological personality constructs that form the basis for classic expressions of leadership such as formulating a vision or motivating by inspiration. Comparative studies of leaders and non-leaders have found that leaders are characterized by a lower level of anxiety and more of an internal locus of control – that is to say, a greater tendency to attribute to themselves the ability to change things in reality. They are more optimistic, which enables them to see the future in a more positive light and consequently to formulate a vision. They have better skills in interpersonal communication and greater faith in their ability to influence others.[13]

In addition to the increased ability to characterize leaders' personality profiles, developments in knowledge on personality permit the investigation of a topic that was discussed by Plato in his day – the development of leaders. In the absence of researchable concepts, this area was ignored for many years, but now, in recent years, scholars are paying more attention to these aspects, and there are growing attempts to examine how the psychological abilities and motivation of individuals who become leaders develop.[14] This research area is still in its infancy but there is increasing evidence of its growth.

In conclusion, it may be said that the psychological research on leaders has shifted from simplistic attempts to classify leaders or leadership styles and examine their differential influence to more complex studies that see leadership as a dependent variable to be studied in more dynamic and developmental terms. This process parallels the development of theoretical and methodological knowledge in general psychology. However, we should bear in mind that dealing with leaders themselves is not the sole purpose of studying the leadership phenomenon, and, in fact, many see this as an unsatisfactory approach and even oppose the centrality ascribed to the personality and place of the leader. Hence, we will now turn to a brief review of other perceptions of the subject.

LEADERSHIP AS AN EXPRESSION OF
THE CIRCUMSTANCES

Karl Marx and Friedrich Engels are probably the most prominent representatives of the approach that is diametrically opposed to the great man approach. "The fact that just this personality and not another appears at a certain time in a certain country is purely accidental," write Marx and Engels, "but if we remove this accident – the need will arise to fill that place and in the course of time someone will be found to fill the role. It was no accident that precisely that Corsican, Napoleon, became the military dictator who was needed by the war-weary French Republic. But if it were not Napoleon, someone else would have taken his place. And the proof is: every time there was a need, a suitable person was always found: Caesar, Augustus, Cromwell, and so forth."[15]

This question – of the relative weight of the leader's personality – has for a long time exercised historians, who are divided on the subject. Many see the rise (and fall) of leaders as a result of circumstances. Some scholars have found, for example, that a crisis situation carries the major weight in the choice of leaders. The rise of leaders such as Winston Churchill or Hitler was explained by researchers and historians as an outcome of the special dynamic created in a severe situation. Also, social psychologists, who performed research manipulations of crisis situations in groups, found that leaders possess much greater influence in crisis periods than at other times, and groups tend to replace their leader with a new one if the former does not have a clear solution to the problem.[16]

This was the form of thinking that was at the basis of the main trend in leadership research in psychology in the 1950s and 1960s. The argument common to most of the models was that the leader is a response to a given situation, a response that stems from the special characteristics of that situation. Some argued that different situations require different leaders, whereas others argued that it is the leadership styles that have to change with the changing circumstances. For example, one scholar who researched leadership in organizations argued that different stages in the life of an organization or different tasks require different types of leaders.[17] It was illustrated that in the early stages of a high-tech organization the leader has to be enterprising, original, development minded, and people oriented. However, if that organization reaches a stage when the focus of the major task changes and what is needed in the new circumstances is to deal less with developing technology and more with marketing, finance, and organization of the system, the new situation calls for a completely different type of leader from the enterprising type who was so suitable in the early stages of development.

In the debate between scholars over the weight of the situational variables, there were some who maintained that the situational variable (as the independent variable) exclusively determines who will be leaders. Thus, some researchers examined the effect of the seating arrangements in groups on leadership status. They showed that when discussion groups of research participants were artificially seated in ways that gave some of them advantages over their friends in terms of ability to communicate (e.g., star-shaped seating, chain seating, wheel), those who were at the junctions of communications tended to adopt leader-like behaviors. This categorical claim was somewhat refined by other scholars, some of whom examined leadership in organizations and argued that changes in the situation did indeed require a change of leader, but the characteristics of the leader had to suit in advance the characteristics of the new situation. Thus, these scholars presented a kind of "engineering" approach that saw the situation as the point of departure, but said that the leader's ability to have effective influence depended on the accuracy in choosing the right leader for the specific situation.[18] Other scholars were less deterministic in the leader-situation context and saw the key to the leader's success in his ability to change his approach and style to match the changing circumstances. This view is not different in essence; it simply gives more credit to the leaders' ability to change according to the requirements of different circumstances. This perception was especially popular in journals that dealt with practical aspects of leadership in organizations.[19] One way or another, it may be said that despite the differences between theorists and researchers of the "situation," they share the same assumptions that the leader is merely a kind of response, he is in fact "a man for all seasons," and it is the times that dictate the type of leader that is required. It may be said, therefore, that despite the differences in the models used in this approach, they all agree that the leader's personality is not the main explanation for events.

Recently there has been an important change in the study of leadership, with scholars arguing that understanding of the leadership phenomenon is not related solely to the personality of the leader or to the characteristics of a given situation. Those who create the different forms and manifestations of leadership, claims one of the radical scholars, are the followers.[20] They build the leader in their consciousness; therefore, we need to understand these mental processes in order to understand the meaning of leadership. Real leadership theory, according to these scholars, is not "theory on leaders" but "theory on followers." Therefore, we will now examine the sources and development of this approach.

LEADERSHIP AS A SUBJECTIVE CREATION OF THE FOLLOWERS

Max Weber, one of the greatest sociologists, made a vital contribution to the discussion on leadership from the point of view of the interpretation of the followers. His discussion on leadership emerged from his general criticism of the methodologies that were then popular in the social sciences. According to Weber, research in the social sciences cannot be based on discovering objective rules that permit precise prediction. The methodology of the social sciences, in Weber's view, is based on the observation of a reality that, by definition, has subjective dimensions and, therefore, must take into account the subjective meanings, the intentions, and the interpretations given to a social situation by the participants in that situation. This contribution of Weber's considerably expanded the discussion on leadership, particularly through his use of the term charisma. According to Weber's point of view, the charismatic leader is one who is **perceived** by his followers as having exceptional qualities and as someone bearing a new message.

Weber's emphasis on the followers' subjective perception of the leader represents a totally different stance from that of Carlyle and the traits scholars, who saw the leader as someone with outstanding objective characteristics, qualities of genius. According to Weber, it is the followers who determine the greatness of the leader and his characteristics. As he put it: "The term 'charisma' will be applied to a certain quality of an individual personality by virtue of which he is set apart from ordinary men and treated as endowed with supernatural, superhuman or at least specifically exceptional powers and qualities. These are such as are not accessible to the ordinary person, but are regarded as exemplary, and on the basis of them the individual concerned is treated as a leader."[21]

This type of explanation – the followers' perceptions – can cast new light on the historical examples mentioned earlier. Ian Kershaw, who spent many years studying what is known as the Hitler enigma, writes in the introduction to his comprehensive book on the subject: "If there is one concept that helped me more than others to integrate various approaches (to the study of Hitler's leadership), it is the concept 'charismatic leadership' as articulated by Max Weber."[22] As quoted previously, Weber seeks explanations for "charisma" in society and not only in the personality of the object of their adulation.

This angle of vision led many writers to deal with processes of "construction" of leaders by the followers. The attempt to understand the followers' dynamic formation or perception of leaders resorted to a broad range of theories, from cognitive psychological theories on processing of information, through theories on consciousness building based on emotional processes, to theories dealing with cultural and anthropological aspects.

The cognitive psychological theories emphasize attribution processes as central in constructing the image of the leader. A typical argument in these studies is that the attribution of leadership to a certain individual is derived from universal processes of information processing. Like the interpretation of many aspects of reality through stimuli and clues that are filled out by cognitive psychological processes to form a complete picture, so it is with leadership. Certain clues (e.g., resolute behavior, decisive speech) create inferences of leadership in the followers' construction of information about the leader.[23]

Other writers on leadership, basing themselves on theories like those of Freud and his followers, which emphasize the centrality of the affective world, see the followers' creation of leaders as a result of emotional processes, some of which are not on the conscious level. For example, there are some who regard the creation of the leader as a projective expression (projection is an unconscious process) of the yearning for an "early father," yearning, imprinted from childhood, for the figures of protective parents. According to this view, there are some people who have characteristics that are perceived as more "parental" because it is easier to project leadership images onto them than onto others.[24] Other scholars see the creation of the leader as an unconscious expression of other internal processes such as narcissism; that is to say, projection onto another that strengthens the follower by virtue of this emotional attachment. According to such perceptions, the characteristics of the leader in the "objective" independent sense are unimportant. The important thing in creating the leader is the psychological characteristics of the followers. An individual may be perceived as a leader if he can serve as the psychological hook on which to hang the followers' narcissistic projections. Paradoxically, vague stimuli create more possibilities for projection.[25]

The concepts of attribution and projection, which are universal in their original theoretical meaning, were expanded to cultural and social contexts. For example, scholars who investigate cultural differences between collectives claim that one of the expressions of intercultural differences is the difference in the prototypes of what is considered good leadership. Thus, a person who is perceived as a leader in one culture will not necessarily be regarded as such in another. Intercultural differences in the perception of leadership are explained, among other things, by psychodynamic arguments such as different attitudes to authority that have been found in comparative studies on national cultures.[26] Be that as it may, beyond the various possible contexts and the additional variables in specific models, the common factor of all these studies is the followers' perception. By examining similarities or differences, the research attempts to identify the psychological rule that governs the construction of the leader in the minds of the followers.

In conclusion, we see that each of the theoretical points of departure presented here a priori emphasizes the power of a certain set of variables to predict or explain the leadership phenomenon. Thus, the discussion and research on leadership are biased from the start. This point will be further expanded and demonstrated in the next chapter and it is the basis for the critical discussion, leading later in the book to a more dynamic and integrative view of this phenomenon that we call leadership.

Chapter 3

✦

Analysis of the Main Perspectives on Leadership

BIASES IN ANALYSIS OF THE LEADERSHIP

On Israel's fiftieth Independence Day, Uri Avneri, a senior Israeli journalist and one of the harshest and most untiring critics of every successive government in Israel, devoted a front-page article to David Ben Gurion. Under the heading "A unique figure in his time,"[1] Avneri summarized David Ben Gurion's biography, his political genius, and above all his concentration on the major effort of establishing the state of Israel while deliberately ignoring all the other events that occurred in those dramatic years. The general impression received when reading the article is that the birth of the state was the accomplishment of a single leader, whose determination shaped the historic circumstances.

This kind of analysis is typical of most of the literature on leadership. This is how leaders, such as Ataturk, Lenin, George Washington, and others who came to be called "fathers of the nation" are described, which emphasized their uniqueness in the historic process. But also leaders who do not belong to the category of "fathers of the nation," such as Churchill, Roosevelt, and even Mussolini and Hitler, are generally attributed with exclusive or decisive importance in the unfolding of events of their period. The eighteenth-century Scottish philosopher Carlyle stated that history is simply the "biography of leaders."[2] "Human history," said Carlyle, "is the chronicle of all the acts committed by man, it is fundamentally the chronicle of the great people who acted in it. Those great people were the leaders of people, they were the creators of everything produced by humanity"

(p. 3). According to Carlyle, a leader's influence is not restricted to the social and political level; a leader is also a spiritual leader. Therefore, Carlyle enumerates among his heroes leaders and prophets whose major characteristic is genius. Carlyle's hero stands head and shoulders above all the others in integrity, courage, originality, and perception.

Is this really so? Is it really true, as Carlyle says, that history is the biography of leaders who shaped it according to their wishes and whims? The answer appears to be much more complex, but before we can fathom its complexity we must first attempt to find some order in that bias that magnifies leaders, sometimes even deifies them.

First, there is **period bias**. This refers to people's tendency to forget that theories and models, particularly in the social context, are formulated by human beings on the basis of the reality they see and experience, and therefore may contain elements that are not necessarily valid for periods other than the ones in which these scholars lived. For example, Malthus,[3] who lived in eighteenth-century Europe, saw thousands of people dying of starvation, because there was not enough food. Clearly, it was this daily reality that led him to formulate his famous theory (which influenced Darwin's thinking) that population growth is much more rapid than the growth of food sources, and therefore "only the strong will survive." Presumably Malthus would not have formulated this theory if he had witnessed the destruction of food surpluses in order to maintain the price level for farmers, a common occurrence today in developed countries, where 3 percent of the population produces a surplus of food.

But why go back to the eighteenth century? Charles Dickens described pitiful scenes of children working from morning till night on production lines. Karl Marx's Communist Manifesto[4] is simply a theoretical formulation based on the reality portrayed by Dickens, whereby those owning the means of production exploited the workers, who were alienated from their work and had "nothing to lose but their chains." Is this the theory that Marx would have formulated if he had constantly seen young people stipulating their agreement to work for a particular company on the promise that they would receive ownership options before even starting the job? Would he have chosen "alienation" as a central concept in his theory if he had constantly seen around him "workaholics" who often took their work home even against the wishes of the management?

Psychological theories dealing with individuals and their motivations are also influenced by the spirit of the period. For example, Freudian theory, which still has great influence in the western world almost 100 years after it was first proposed, underwent revisions in the formulation of neo-Freudian approaches, which may be attributed to the changing times. Freud, who grew up in Vienna of the late-nineteenth-century, like most children at that time saw his father as a remote, perhaps even frightening, figure, whom one addressed as "sir." The father was not a person with whom one played football, tumbled around on the carpet, or played electric trains. With this kind of father-son relationship it was only natural that Freudian theory should place so much weight on the superego. The fact is that the theories of later psychoanalysts, especially the Americans among them, place much less emphasis on the superego, the "entity" that is responsible for moral judgments, for deciding what is forbidden and what is permitted.[5]

The same general argument applies to theories and models of leadership. What did Carlyle see in the nineteenth century and in the periods preceding it? He saw kings' courts, princes, aristocrats, knights and warriors, and eminent artists. Most of the population was oppressed and cowed, lacking all rights and clearly not participants in shaping historical processes. Wars and conquests, as well as the cultural and artistic activities of figures such as Leonardo da Vinci or Michelangelo, were conducted through the courts of kings and barons. In such circumstances, it was impossible to reach any other conclusion than that expressed by Carlyle. However, this reality has changed and continues to change dramatically since the "spring of nations."

James MacGregor Burns[6] claims that most historical writers in fact describe **rulers** rather than **leaders**. Rulers can force their people to act because they control resources and possess military power, because their people attribute to them divine power rooted in tradition, or because of other objective and subjective factors that endow them with concrete or potential power to intimidate their followers. Rulers could build castles for their mistresses and execute insubordinate people with impunity. Leadership, on the other hand, according to most theoreticians of the democratic era, is not based on force or formal authority, but on influence that stems from elements in the personality, outlook, and behavior of the leader as these are reflected in the eyes of the followers. The theme of "psychological influence" is common to most definitions of leadership.[7] For example, John Kotter,[8] a leadership scholar from Harvard, sees leadership as making people act without using means of coercion (as distinct from making them act out of fear of force, sanctions, and so forth). A similar view was presented by Ruth Willner, who studied the influence of charismatic leaders, and reached the conclusion that leadership is simply "voluntary patterns of influence."[9] General Dwight Eisenhower, interestingly in light of his being a military man, emphasized the difference between leadership and other ways of inducing people to act. He said that leadership means making people **want** to act, causing them to act out of a feeling that the decisions are theirs alone.[10] And indeed, current leadership theory and research place increasing emphasis on the followers. It appears that, at least from the point of view of leadership scholars, the time has passed when the leader was the only element in the formula. Now the followers have become a major component in the analysis of leadership.

However, analysis of leadership from the point of view of the followers reveals that the followers are often biased in the direction of "magnification" of the leaders due to a tendency known in cognitive psychology as the **fundamental attribution error**. This is a bias whereby people tend to see behavior as deriving from the characteristics of the performer and to minimize, or even ignore, the influence of situational factors. A well-known experiment by Ross and associates[11] illustrates the strength of the fundamental attribution error. The researchers conducted a quiz among their subjects. The participants were divided arbitrarily into two groups: "questioners" and "contestants." The questioners were instructed to find particularly hard questions; they were entitled to ask questions on subjects that the other team could not possibly know. An audience observed the allocation of roles and the quiz, and they knew that the role distribution was random. Nevertheless, they attributed more knowledge to the questioners than to the contestants and ignored the fact that the questioners' advantage stemmed solely from the role assigned to them at random. In other words, anyone could have successfully filled the role of questioner and gained the advantage.

Instances of this cognitive bias can be seen daily in newspaper reports and articles. For example, regular public opinion polls, and even analysis by various experts, of the public's trust in senior role-bearers, such as the U.S. president, and the public's perception of their functioning, indicate that the trend of trust rises substantially **after** the president is elected to office. There are examples showing that shifts in the American economy resulting from external changes were attributed to the president elect before he had even had time to enter upon his office and make any decisions.[12] People tend to think that if he is the president (or the prime minister or the chief of staff) he must be a leader, otherwise he would never have reached that position. In the same way, many believe that the radical changes in the Soviet Union in the early 1990s were the **exclusive** work of Gorbachev. They simply ignore the circumstances of poverty and corruption and the awareness that had already begun to develop among conservatives, such as Andropov, that "the system doesn't work," an awareness shared by most members of the Politburo. This unconscious bias, the fundamental attribution error, merits further discussion.

A fascinating example of the fundamental attribution error appears in the famous novel, *Being There*, by the Polish-American writer, Jerzy Kosinski.[13] The protagonist of the novel is a man called Chance – an ignorant and mentally retarded gardener who had worked all his life on the estate of an old man. When he was not tending the garden he spent his time in his room, obsessively watching mindless television programs, attempting to imitate the facial expressions and behavior of the characters in the programs.

One day the old man, Chance's benevolent patron, died, and he was thrown out into the world beyond the estate. Until then his patron had taken care of him and prevented him from being sent to an institution. Now he was left completely defenseless. Chance left the boundaries of the estate for the first time and was hit by a limousine. As he was only slightly injured, the owner of the limousine, Mrs. Rand, wife of the chairman of a huge American concern, took him home with her. She soon became deeply impressed by Chance's rare intelligence and insight. In actual fact, the only thing Chance did in his conversations with Mrs. Rand was to repeat what she had said – a form of response he had learned from the TV programs he watched.

Mrs. Rand was not the only one who was impressed by Chance, the feeble-minded gardener. Her husband, too, a businessman with a finger in every pie, was deeply impressed by Chance's wisdom. When Rand asked Chance about his business, the following conversation took place: "It's not easy, sir," said Chance, "There are not many chances of getting a good garden where you can work undisturbed and cultivate it according to the changing seasons." Mr. Rand leaned toward him smugly and said, "Extremely well put, a gardener, uh? Isn't that a wonderfully apt description of a true businessman? A person who tills the soil with his sweat, waters the ground and harvests from it worthwhile products for his family, his community. Yes, Chance! What a wonderful metaphor! Indeed, a productive businessman is like a man of the soil, cultivating his vine" (pp. 33–4).

The process of attributing superior wisdom to the ignorant gardener gathered momentum. The president of the United States, who visited occasionally to consult with business magnate Rand, came to the house and talked with Chance. He took the opportunity to ask Chance's opinion about the rough period in the U.S. economy. Chance replied, "There are always seasons in gardening. There is spring, there is summer, but there is also fall and winter, and then again spring and summer. So long as the roots are not seriously damaged, everything is all right." The U.S. president took Chance's words as one of the wisest and most optimistic statements he had ever heard and began to use Chance's metaphor of the "seasons" in his senate speeches.

From then on, things snowballed. One thing led to another, and Chance suddenly found himself appearing on a TV show. Introducing the program, the host noted that the U.S. president compared the American economy to a garden. Chance, when he was invited to speak, simply recited the only thing he knew and had done all his life. "I know the garden well," he said firmly, "I have worked at this job all my life, the good, healthy garden. The trees are healthy, and so are the flowers and the other plants. And they will stay that way if they are watered and treated properly according to the seasons of the year. The garden needs proper care. I agree with the U.S. president. There is room for new trees and new flowers of different kinds. . ." And so Chance went on, describing the garden he had worked in on the old man's estate. "In the garden the plants grow, but you also have to go through the fall, the trees shed their leaves and their color changes. It is a stage in the process of becoming taller and thicker. True, some branches die, but others grow in their place. If you like the garden it is not hard to wait. And then, in the right season, you see the blossom." The audience responded enthusiastically to Chance's "profound" words. They all wanted to meet him and get to know him. When he laughed without rhyme or reason at the Russian ambassador's reception, the latter immediately suspected that Chance knew Russian and had overheard a joke someone had told in that language. When journalists asked him what newspapers he preferred to read, Chance replied that he did not read any paper (in fact he couldn't read or write). "I watch TV programs all the time," he said spontaneously. The admiration for him grew; this reply came across as one of the most honest answers ever uttered by a public figure. Later he became a public idol; he was chosen as "best dressed man." All the papers wanted to write front-page stories about him. And thus Kosinski wittily portrays the human need (which has been defined by some as a fundamental one) to create authority figures, to create leaders.

The process whereby the followers construct leadership figures is a major subject of interest in the psychological literature on leadership, particularly during the past decade. If we look for a moment at the literary example presented earlier, we can see it as an example (albeit extreme) of "inventing a character" in people's awareness. The character is not invented on the basis of thorough acquaintance, exceptional actions, impressive rhetorical skills, or even on distinguished outward appearance. Many explanations have been offered at various levels of discussion and based on diverse disciplines and approaches, from cognitive psychology through psychodynamic processes to anthropological explanations. I will review the major arguments here.

Cognitive psychologists (who deal with mental functions such as processing of information in general and of social information in particular) refer to concepts such as "heuristics" (rules of thinking, interpreting, and judging), schemata, prototypes, and similar mental constructs that help the individual to "interpret the world." This is an active process, based on cues that the individual receives, processes, and adopts as the groundwork for judgment, decisions, or behavior. In these terms, the question is not who is the leader but what type of cues do people have to receive in order to attribute leadership qualities to a certain person.

The example of Chance demonstrates some processes that have been discussed in research. For example, the scholars Conger and Kanungo[14] argue that determined, assertive behavior is conducive to the attribution of leadership. Chance's clear, decisive speech (although it is really meaningless) enables people to pick up the cue that he is indeed a leader. In addition, the attribution process is influenced by various items of information entering people's awareness. For instance, the fact that Chance was seen as the friend of a financial magnate, who in turn, was a friend and advisor to the President of the United States, supported the attribution of leadership. Furthermore, this process involves a phenomenon defined by scholars as "social contagion."[15] As with a contagious disease, people transmit to each other attributions of leadership, relay stories, and supply information that is not always accurate until finally a "character is built." As in the case of Chance, it may be that the individual in question did not make any deliberate efforts to be recognized as a leader. The story of Chance is a fictional one, but reality affords many examples that are not too far from this description.

Shamir[16] shows that such processes are intensified by distance from the leader. The greater the distance and the less direct the contact with the leader, the easier it is to turn him into a subjective creation. In a study conducted by Shamir, 320 students at the Hebrew University of Jerusalem were asked to choose two types of leaders: a close leader, with whom they had personal contact (those chosen for this category were typically youth movement leaders, military commanders, or school teachers) and a distant leader, one with whom they never had close contact (typical leaders in this group were Menachem Begin, Ben-Gurion). The subjects' attitudes toward the two categories of leaders were collected through interviews. In general it was found that the distant leaders were perceived in a much more stereotyped manner as figures larger than life possessing characteristics different from those of close leaders. The general conclusion is that close contact with the leader turns him into a creature of flesh and blood with vices and virtues rather than a stereotyped attribution.

A scene I recall from a Japanese movie provides a good illustration of this argument. In the movie Japanese soldiers are shown trudging along wearily after a fierce battle. Their utter exhaustion is visible in every motion; they are barely capable of moving. Reaching a certain spot in a canyon, they raise their heads and see their leader standing on the hilltop and waving them on to their next battle. Their reaction is instantaneous. They stand erect, their eyes glow with eagerness, and their footsteps become brisk as they march into battle. The impact of the leader's presence is undeniable. Then the camera zooms in to the leader standing on the hilltop with his hand stretched upwards, and in the close-up we see that he is dead. Somebody is holding him up from behind and waving his hand. The entire emotional effect is the creation of the followers.

Apparently some of the more charismatic leaders in history, including the most destructive ones – such as Jim Jones, the leader of a sect whose charismatic influence persuaded 911 of his followers to commit suicide, or Hitler, who swept millions along with him – intuitively sensed the psychological effect of distance.[17] Jim Jones held confessional sessions with his people in darkness from a distance that made it hard to see him. He certainly guarded what sociologists call "social distance." Hitler took care to be photographed in propaganda films from an angle that made him look taller, stronger, and more militant.

A salient example of the effect of distance is the mythologization of Yitzhak Rabin after his assassination. Beyond his image as an honest man, Rabin was a controversial figure during his lifetime. Both as chief of staff and as prime minister in his first term of office he was criticized as being indecisive. In his second term, there were other criticisms of his leadership. Regardless of whether the criticism was justified, the dynamics can be seen clearly. The further the distance from the living Rabin, the more he became a mythical leader unparalleled by anyone other than the "founding father" – David Ben Gurion.[18]

Finally, the cultural aspect has an impact on attributions of leadership. Comparative studies conducted by sociologists[19] found various intercultural differences in values, which may be summarized in three spheres: 1) the attitude to authority; 2) the individual's self-perception, particularly with regard to two dimensions: the relationship between the individual and society, and the individual's self-perception with regard to masculinity and femininity; and 3) ways of expressing emotions. The studies show that there are peoples (such as the Chinese or Arabs) whose attitude to authority is one of distance and respect as a result of their socialization. In other societies (e.g., in Scandinavian countries) the relations between parents and children are closer and more direct. Therefore, the attitude to authority figures is closer. Some nations are more "masculine," with a clear division between male and female roles; the men are the wage-earners, whereas the women are responsible for taking care of the family. And there are more egalitarian societies, such as Sweden, where the role divisions between men and women are almost completely obliterated. Similarly, differences were found with regard to individualism and collectivism. For example, American society emphasizes the centrality of the individual in the socialization of children, whereas the Druse place the community – the village and the tribe – at the center of the socialization process. Societies also differ in the extent of their tolerance of uncertainty. Some, like the German society, are very orderly and have rules and regulations designed to prevent uncertainty, which is highly threatening to them, as illustrated by Hofstede,[20] a researcher on cultures, whereas other societies are more tolerant of uncertainty and less orderly. These differences are significant in terms of the perception and attribution of leadership, as borne out by studies conducted on prototypes of leadership in various cultures.[21] For example, Gerstner and Day[22] compared perceptions of leadership among populations of students in eight countries. They asked the students to grade fifty-nine characteristics of leadership that had been identified in various studies and found very little agreement among the students concerning these characteristics. It was not possible to identify core leadership images on which there was clear agreement. Moreover, of the first five leadership traits graded in the American sample not one was found in the top five places in the other samples.

The main problem with such studies is that the subjects generally arrive at their views by looking at leaders known to them from their own country and culture, and naturally these figures themselves may differ substantially from each other. Thus, the followers' views in an inter-cultural comparison may reflect differences between the leaders themselves rather than perceptions of leadership prototypes.

A recent Israeli study attempted to overcome these limitations. Conducted in a factory, the study examined workers' leadership perceptions regarding **the same** manager.[23] This research design made it possible to isolate the possible differences between the leaders themselves and to focus on the followers' perceptions and attributions of leadership *per se*. The difference between the followers was cultural; some of them were new immigrants from the former Soviet Union and some were indigenous Israelis or old-timers. The subjects were paired for matching in terms of background variables. For example, a thirty-eight-year-old Russian worker with a secondary education who was married and a father of two was paired with an Israeli old-timer of similar age, education, and family status. This procedure was followed in order to ensure that only the effect of cultural differences on perceptions of leadership would be examined. The findings do indeed reveal differences in the perception of the same leader. In general, immigrants from the former Soviet Union were found to have more respect for authority and hence different leadership prototypes.

Some other explanations for followers' tendencies to "magnify" the leader are related to the dynamics existing in the typical family where big strong adults take care of helpless babies. In other words, the longing for a big, strong, protective figure is ingrained in us as a primary, instinctive pattern. The core of this explanation is the psychological mechanism (on which I will elaborate later) known as **projection**. According to the *Dictionary of Psychoanalysis*,[24] projection is "a process whereby certain aspects of the self, such as desires and urges, are found in (projected onto) an object (another person) outside the self." By its very nature, this mechanism enables the subject to project desires onto the figures of strangers. This is a possible explanation for the adulation of glamorous actors, as well as for the wish to find leaders who can be magnified and made "great." A type of projection that is relevant to the discussion on leadership was defined by Freud as **transference**, which occurs when an individual perceives another and responds to him as if he were a dominant figure from his past (e.g., a father). The leader, according to Freud, embodies "parental representations" in the followers' consciousness, representations that sometimes surpass the real life figure, which is thus easy to magnify.[25]

As opposed to Carlyle and others like him, who saw the leader, his personality, his decisions, and his behaviors as the essence of the entire leadership phenomenon, the analysis presented earlier views the followers as the exclusive creators of the leader. It is all in their minds; they create the leader, take him to their hearts, and magnify him according to their needs, longings, and expectations. They mold the leader in their awareness. Therefore, according to this argument, every theory of leadership is really a theory of "followership," and in order to understand the leadership phenomenon we need to focus on the dynamics among the followers. There are some scholars who believe that this is the approach appropriate to the study of leadership as a psychological phenomenon, both at the personal and social level.[26]

However, just as it may be argued that an approach focusing on the leader alone is narrow, one-dimensional, and overly romantic, a similar objection might be put forward with regard to an approach that focuses exclusively on the followers. Churchill was perceived as a great leader in wartime Britain, yet the same British followers did not consider him a suitable leader when the national mission changed from war to restoring the British economy and society. Moshe Dayan was the most venerated leader in Israel in a period when existential anxieties were at the center of the Israeli public consciousness, but when he decided to run for the parliament some years later, he did not sweep the public along with him. Truman came to the presidency as a gray figure after the death of the charismatic Roosevelt; yet, contrary to all expectations, he became an outstanding and esteemed leader. Anwar Sadat was at first ridiculed by the Egyptians, who had totally revered Abdul Nasser, but he became a great Egyptian leader. There are examples of leaders, such as Gandhi or Nelson Mandela, who changed their followers' awareness instead of being enslaved to it. There were people who failed to be accepted as leaders at the beginning of their careers, but were accepted later (Richard Nixon, Winston Churchill). At less exalted levels there are innumerable examples of leaders who succeeded with one group of followers and not with another. In organizations of various kinds there are examples of managers/leaders who succeeded at one hierarchical level, but did not prove so successful at another level.[27] Thus we see that leadership is far too complicated to be seen from a dichotomous or static perspective. It is a dynamic psychological phenomenon, affected by changes in the situation and the tasks at hand, in the leaders' outlooks and behaviors, and in the followers' tendencies and perceptions. Because leadership is dynamic, it should be defined in dynamic terms. The appropriate conceptual framework for this is the view of leadership as **relationship**, and it is from this point of view that we will examine it.

LEADERSHIP AS RELATIONSHIP

The view of leadership as a dynamic relationship not only includes both leaders and followers in the formula, but also assumes that each side contributes to the dynamics. In other words, relationships are dynamic interactions forming a psychological essence that may change in response to circumstances or to changes occurring in the leaders or among the followers. Therefore, I will describe here the various types of relationships between leaders and followers and the typical conditions necessary for the existence of the different types.

The most basic distinction in human relationships is the distinction between relations based on rationality and those based on emotions. This is one of the most basic distinctions in the discussion of human nature in general.[28] The major concept that is used to explain the "rational dynamic" existing between the leader and the followers is the concept of **exchange**.[29]

All the scholars and researchers who base their work on this concept argue that interpersonal relations are similar in essence to business relationships, in the sense that these relations are expected to satisfy both sides, and that, in fact, is a condition for their existence. In the absence of such conditions, or when changes occur in the terms of the agreement, the relationship naturally ceases to exist or has to be redefined. Rational leader-follower relations are based on the assumption that both sides, the leader and the followers, are rational and fully aware of their decisions and choices. Therefore, the relationship between them is freely chosen and serves the interests of both sides. Such relations are defined as instrumental relations, that is to say, they further interests that can be defined and sometimes actually measured in terms of cost benefit (according to the definitions of cost and benefit prevalent in the society in question).[30] Indeed, the view of human nature in terms of "economic rationality" was the point of departure for the construction of some models that provided the theoretical basis for leadership research for many years.[31] However, these rational models cannot explain, for example, why people risk their lives to save someone they don't know or are prepared to give money (often secretly) to a cause they believe in or fight for an idea. The models also cannot explain why people devote their time and money to ideological issues or demonstrate for a cause freely over long periods, often without recognition from society or even a word of thanks. Clearly, human desires and actions are more complex than those described in instrumental models. This has been shown by scholars and researchers[32] who have found, for example, that people have needs for belonging[33] and for meaning.[34] In other words, people are also motivated by needs that psychological literature calls "affective." They want to feel that they are doing something bigger than themselves and to be part of something more ideological. Moreover, as will be shown later, the actors are sometimes completely unaware of the motives underlying many of their aspirations and behaviors, which are motives that are not given to analysis in conventional terms of cost benefit.

Nevertheless, a broad range of leader-follower relations can be characterized with the help of models based on the affective explanation, including relationships of pathological dependence leading to suicide at the leader's request, as in the case of Jim Jones,[35] or of outstanding ethical behavior that can be attributed to the influence of a leader, as manifested in the case of Mahatma Gandhi.[36] Using the major psychological theories concerning emotions, we can roughly describe three types of emotional relationships existing between leaders and followers: regressive relationships, developmental relationships, and symbolic relationships. The nature of these three types of relationships will be described subsequently.

LEADERS AND FOLLOWERS: REGRESSIVE RELATIONSHIPS

Regressive relations have their roots in two psychological mechanisms that were mentioned earlier: projection[37] and transference.[38] The basic dynamics set in motion through these mechanisms may be demonstrated in the common phenomenon of falling in love. The individual falling in love often sees in the beloved someone quite different from the real person. Many characteristics are magnified and less agreeable ones are played down or even ignored completely. Thus, the lover often sees a figure that is entirely a figment of his imagination. It is well known that in many cases this subjective and sometimes totally idealized picture of the beloved changes after a time, and suddenly those characteristics that were not seen before "appear." What is the explanation for this phenomenon in which certain figures acquire a particular image (usually enlarged and flattering) in some people's eyes? How can persons who appear in a certain light look so different in a different period or different circumstances? How can there be such distortions in perception and judgment? The evidence that we possess from cases and studies that have been described in clinical psychological literature indicates some distinctive features in these processes, the basic elements of which are not conscious at all (on the part of the lover in this example). Nevertheless, there is some order whose source lies in the psychological structure of the one who "paints the picture," which sometimes unconsciously influences his/her decisions and emotional attachments.

Analysis (usually retrospective) of romantic relations often reveals motives that can be identified in the personal history of the lover, even though she or he may not have been aware of this while falling in love.[39] Some of the evidence indicates that the lover (again, unconsciously) reproduces relationships with a parent, sometimes in an attempt to "revive" relationships from the past or to compensate for bad relationships. Whichever the case, these internal desires are projected onto the other. Therefore, in order to understand the sources of the "creation" of the other, it is necessary to understand and analyze the internal world of the projector, the creator of the image.

Projective relations exist not only between people in love, they may well exist between followers and their leader. In point of fact, Freud saw leadership in these terms. He writes:

It is the longing for a father which is common to all humans from their childhood days. Now it may become clear to us that the characteristics that we attribute to the great person are the characteristics of parents, and that the essence of the greatness of great people lies in this convention. Resoluteness, strength of will, and energetic action are part of the picture of the father.[40]

In other words, the leader is not necessarily a real figure, but a figment of the followers' (perhaps unconscious) longing and desires. This naturally raises the question as to why the projections of many people, sometimes thousands and even millions, are directed to one particular person. This will be discussed later.

But what about the leader himself? As mentioned, the literature on the psychology of leadership has barely touched on this aspect, largely due to methodological difficulties. However, returning to the metaphor of falling in love, there is no doubt that the leader plays a complementary and sustaining part in these relations. Usually it is a question of reciprocal dynamics of emotional needs. There is no lack of evidence to illustrate these reciprocal relations. The better-known cases in terms of psychological research are in religious sects or in protest groups, some of them violent. The extreme manifestation of the phenomenon is presented here not as a generalization but simply to illustrate the point that the true dynamics underlying intense (sometimes pathological) emotional relationships are not always visible on the surface. Often, these attachments are incomprehensible to the outside observer, yet deeper analysis reveals an intense emotional relationship whose sources lie in a history that generated certain emotional needs and structures.

The case of the Charles Manson gang[41] illustrates this argument clearly. Manson headed a gang known as "the Manson family," which became notorious at the end of the 1960s, after murdering a group of people at a party in Los Angeles. The Manson family occupied the minds of the American public to a disproportionate extent. This interest, as far as one can judge, stemmed not only from the horrific murders but also, and perhaps mainly, from the background of Manson's followers, which was so different from his own. Apart from Manson himself, all the gang members came from wealthy, educated families, which were typical representatives of the middle and upper classes. They were not miserable and destitute outcasts with nothing to lose, but young people who had received the best of education and had a guaranteed future. Thus, the question as to what caused them to follow Manson so blindly and totally is a complex psychological and sociological question that touches on basic issues in American education.

Manson, born in 1934, was a few years older than his followers. Unlike them, he came from a lower class family. In fact, he was born to a family whose condition may be described as chaotic. Abandonment and a sense of illegitimacy were the major characteristics of his childhood. He never knew his father, his mother literally abandoned him as an infant, and he was raised by distant relatives who shunted him from family to family. Therefore, he never lived in a warm, stable framework. The longest period he spent with anyone was with his grandmother, who was an extremely authoritarian figure. There is no doubt that internalization of the sense of abandonment was the dominant factor in his personality, as he later described to his biographer: "I was an outlaw from birth. Rejection, more than love and acceptance, has been a part of my life since birth. . ."[42] As he put it, his mother had neither the desire nor the ability to take the responsibility for raising him. "You might say I was a child that nobody wanted," said Manson in an interview.[43]

Manson had a powerful longing to be accepted, to belong, but, as often happens at the pathological level, what he expressed outwardly was the reverse of these desires. Hatred and suppression of intimate feelings characterized his behavior toward other people. His greatest fear was, in fact, what he had known all his life: disappointment and abandonment. At the age of sixteen he was sent to prison, where he met people whose identity had been shaped by crime, and this he adopted for himself. But even as a thief, he proved to be a failure; he was caught and again imprisoned. On his release, his wife left him; he was again arrested for robbery and sentenced to ten years in jail. And thus, once again Manson found himself abandoned and deserted by everyone he knew in the outside world. The circumstances and the atmosphere of that period (1967), especially in San Francisco, facilitated his readjustment to life outside prison and contributed substantially to his rebirth as "head of a family" and his acceptance by his followers. This played an important part in his remodeling and his acceptance of himself as "head of a family."

At that time, in San Francisco more than anywhere else in the United States, poverty was not considered shameful. People slept in the streets undisturbed, and love, sex, and drugs were free. Nobody paid attention to Manson's past. His hippie appearance and his talent for playing the guitar enabled him to live better than he had in other places. He was then, as he told his biographer, "quite a happy man." All the practices that were later attributed to him, such as taking drugs, he claimed to have learned from his "students." His influence on them was in the perception that was so characteristic of his lifestyle and outlook, summarized in the sentence: "The door is not the way out. The way out is when you don't want to go out any more – only then are you free." The message that a person can free himself spiritually and subjectively fell on fertile ground. His students, especially in light of the background from which they came, liked this message. As one of them described it: "The man himself (Manson) and the journey he had undergone through rejection and suffering to spiritual rebirth was an example to them."[44] Manson in fact reconstructed for the group members the process that he himself had undergone. According to his beliefs, in order to achieve the required spontaneity, people had to experience "psychological and spiritual death, that would break every independent individual and leave him with a dead head."[45]

Manson called this "reprogramming," a process that entailed "peeling off all the false masks." He adopted this attitude under the influence of some books he had read. For example, he was strongly influenced by Eric Berne's *Games People Play*. Berne speaks a great deal about various types of children. One of the types discussed in the book is the "pure child." The creation of such a child was one of Manson's wishes. A child "free of parents," who lives in the present, the moment, and never wonders where he came from and what he was. In a press interview, he said that he used to explain to his believers that life had taught him that "a person has to forget yesterday and who he was before. He should not develop hopes about what tomorrow will bring . . . I agreed with them that they had to get out of the rat race because they would soon become greedier." In the same interview he said: "I began to enjoy the sense of power that I received from those around me, but it was not power as an aim in itself. Do you understand, I enjoyed the fact that I was needed and never felt better."[46] The entire lifestyle of the Manson family was present-oriented. They called each other by nicknames; they did not know their friends' real names or anything about their past. The only one whose life story and real name they knew was Manson. Manson's indoctrination succeeded in generating feelings of joy and happiness in the family members. As one of them described it: "It was love that flowed through your body like thick syrup in your veins, warming wherever it went, making you so 'one' with the person you were with . . . that the distinctions between the two of you hardly existed any more. . . ."

Manson had two prominent characteristics: inner emptiness, from which he found escape in the power he accumulated, and remarkable sensitivity to certain types of distress that he had suffered in his own life, such as loneliness. He needed the group no less than the group needed him. In fact, projecting his feelings onto the group saved him from thoughts of escape and death. As he described it: "I often had the urge to get my things together and head for unknown places, but I was so caught up with those kids and the role I played in their lives, to leave them would have been like ripping my heart out."[47] And thus, the preoccupation with release through death was replaced by the theme of giving, of redeeming tortured souls. But death lurked beneath these rationalizations, and found its expression when the cracks appeared. The first manifestations of this were signs of paranoia. In the state of anxiety (in the clinical sense) that overpowered Manson shortly before the murders, he began to rationalize his fears as an expression of vitality. The family, sunk in total paranoia, which Manson described as total awareness, began to live like a pack of wolves. They began to carry knives, and Manson himself carried a "magic sword." They traveled in roundabout ways and drove very quickly; they practiced stalking and gradually internalized the feeling that they were being hunted. They reached such a highly charged psychological state that they had to do something to release the pressure, otherwise the group would break up. Manson began to picture a catalyzing act that would destroy the forces of darkness and evil so that a new era could begin. The murders that they planned gained legitimacy from the inner logic that developed in the family. Manson's hatred did not fall on deaf ears, because this was what had attracted the group to him in the first place. To them, he represented the opposite of their hated parents – successful, middle class, career-minded people, who were so absorbed in themselves that they had given their children an unbearable experience of marginality. Manson was a counteracting force to their parents' paralyzing power, but they perceived this force as their own. For the first time in their lives, they felt omnipotent, strong, capable of shattering, breaking, and destroying. No power could match them when they were "one" and near Manson. However, Manson had a new theme. This time, rather than being abandoned again, he was prepared to kill and destroy. It was much easier than being destroyed once again. As soon as this awareness and these feelings became rooted in the family spirit, brutal murder was no longer unthinkable, and indeed, it took place a few days later.

Many of the themes in the story of the Manson family are similar to those that appear in the case of Jim Jones, the charismatic leader of a sect who persuaded its members to kill themselves in the largest mass suicide in history. Over 900 people, including scores of children, took their own lives at the request of their leader, Jim Jones. Jones, too, was a lonely and abandoned child who found psychological refuge in his followers' adulation (he had been a priest at a certain stage in his life). As a young boy, he found refuge in fantasies of people obeying him while he was at the center of attention. He, too, felt that life was uncertainty, betrayal, alienation, rejection, and loneliness. All these were relieved temporarily and partially by people's dependence on him and by the omnipotence that was built around this dependence. His inner world was somber, and his feelings often touched upon death. In time, when he was interviewed in jail, he said that in his heart he had been dead for a long time, and it was only his desire to help others who needed him that kept him going. He said to his interviewers: "Ever since as a child I saw a dog die, I wanted to commit suicide. It was the first time I felt guilt. But I still had some little dogs and cats alive, and I had to keep care of them, so I stayed alive... Later my mom needed me, and then some poor souls down the road... It's always been that way."[48]

These two cases demonstrate clearly not just the hidden basis of certain people's strong desire to become leaders, but also the psychological complexity of emotional relations between leaders and followers. In these extreme cases, as the leaders and the followers themselves testified, the relationship was a kind of healing response to the distress of both sides. Researchers who deal with psychological deprivation relevant to the kind described here, which is known in the professional literature as "narcissistic deprivation,"[49] argue that narcissistic deprivation is extremely powerful in motivating people and creating links between them. The cases of Manson and Jones demonstrate how the desires and behaviors of both sides – leaders and followers – stem from such deprivation. (I will elaborate on narcissistic deprivation as a motivational mechanism for leadership in Chapter 5, on the development of leaders.)

The narcissistic explanation centers around a process known as mirroring. The word mirror comes from the Latin root *mirari*, meaning not just to look but also to admire. *Mirari* is also connected with the word mirage, which means optical illusion. A mirror is, therefore, a possible tool both for seeing the truth and for distorting it. A mirror can be a screen on which images are projected. Indeed, this theme is prevalent in many variations in legends, folk tales, and myths. The most famous myth about the mirroring effect is Ovid's story of Narcissus, a beautiful youth who saw his reflection in a pool of water, fell in love with it, and could not tear his eyes away from it until he died of exhaustion – he loved himself to death.

Through mirroring, say scholars of narcissism, the individual creates projections, overcomes inhibitions, and forms his ideas and images. The mirror metaphor suggests a diversity of images, and this may lead to severance between the private and the public awareness (as history has shown). What we want to see and what we fear to see may be completely different worlds. Narcissistic deprivation, like all deprivations, leads to a search for ways to fill the gap; people who suffer from it are busy seeking attention and admiration, and in extreme cases, such as those described previously, are obsessively occupied with this search throughout their entire lives. "I will be famous," wrote Honoré de Balzac to a friend while he was still at school. "My sole desire is to be famous and loved."[50] He achieved both, but that did not prevent him from immersing himself in his writing even when he was famous and highly esteemed. Thus, it appears that, as the British psychoanalyst Anthony Storr pointed out, literary and artistic work are distinctly therapeutic forms of reactions to narcissistic deprivation.[51]

Some leadership scholars claim that leadership, and a certain form of followership, are also possible solutions to narcissistic deprivation. This claim is based on the theoretical arguments of Heinz Kohut, whose theory on the phenomenon of narcissism has strongly influenced the thinking on the subject.[52] According to Kohut, narcissistic deprivation can lead to two compensation processes that are relevant to a certain type of "love affair" between the leader and the followers. Some leaders will develop a tendency to seek followers who will serve as a mirror reflecting wonderment and adoration. In this pattern, narcissistic leaders are "mirror-hungry personalities," namely people whose motivation to lead is based on the wish to find the admiration they so lacked in the early stages of their lives. The followers are thus a possible source of admiration and adulation, and the more submissive and dependent they are the better this serves the leaders' needs for admiration. But because not everyone has the talent or ability to be a leader (as will be explained in Chapter 5), some individuals with narcissistic deprivation become obsessive seekers of figures to admire. These are "ideal-hungry personalities," and when they find such figures, they themselves – through the projective process described earlier – become, in their own eyes, more like the objects of their admiration and thus worth more in their own eyes.

The meeting of mirror-hungry personalities with ideal-hungry personalities creates the dynamics of a love affair in which there is no perception of reality, no outside world, no faults or weaknesses, only desires and fantasies that feed the sometimes pathological needs of both sides. The cases of Manson and Jones demonstrate, at least partially, this category of narcissistic relations. Because this is a "meeting of pathologies," it is clearly a rare occurrence, so these examples and explanations are not given to broad generalization. However, they do illustrate the powerful unconscious processes that underlie certain kinds of leader-follower relations.

Aberbach presents another type of emotional relationship, which also stems from projection and demonstrates reciprocity in the emergence of psychological feelings created solely by desires.[53] He enumerates a list of historical leaders who on the face of it, based, let's say, on a demographic analysis of similarity in vital characteristics, reveal nothing to clarify why people flocked after them. Napoleon was not a pure Frenchman. Born in Corsica, he was of Italian descent. Garibaldi, the revered Italian leader, was a Frenchman, born in Nice, and spoke broken Italian. Hitler was an

Austrian citizen. Robespierre and Lenin were idols of the masses, of the proletariat, but they themselves did not come from this social stratum.

The emotional attachment stems from the perception of the leader as representing a possible solution to deep collective distress. To a defeated and humiliated Germany, Hitler represented the national pride and aggression that had been so crushed by the "knife in the back" legend and Germany's severe economic situation between the two world wars. Lenin represented a solution to the shameful poverty in which millions of destitute people existed. In each case, the followers apparently identified the leader as someone who could solve their collective problems. Aberbach couples together the followers' distress and their attraction to certain leaders, using the general term "trauma." In his opinion, certain people can generate strong emotional communication out of the experience of trauma. There are leaders whose biography testifies to their success in creating for themselves a new identity out of their struggle with the trauma, thus learning to overcome sorrow and pain. They create a kind of mythology of themselves. Jones, the abandoned child, became a priest and saw himself as giving love to people who lacked it. Manson saw himself as rescuing young people from emptiness and a cruel parochial society. Hitler regarded himself as bearing a mission, as the redeemer of the Aryan race. The psychological needs characteristic of trauma situations are served when the unique story of such a leader, who has experienced a certain trauma and learned to overcome it, and above all is familiar with the emotional nuances of these traumatic feelings (which he identifies with the keen intuition that comes from experience), becomes a powerful psychological element. People in a traumatized condition (even if they are not always aware of it) can easily make a certain individual the object of their projections if they perceive him as representing recovery from a trauma similar to their own. Because projection becomes particularly intense in traumatized states, a psychologically rare situation may arise whereby people form emotional attachments that seem incomprehensible on the surface. This may happen in the case of certain types of leaders and followers. Moreover, there are situations in which extreme, even pathological, aspects of the leader's personality, which in everyday life would be considered a severe disadvantage, paradoxically become a source of leadership and of hope and optimism in the eyes of many. Often a long time may pass, and much blood may be shed, before it is finally discovered that the followers were swept along by false hopes and that their optimism was merely wishful thinking.

There are also other explanations of the type of relations described here between leaders and followers,[54] but the main idea seems quite clear. Relations of this type are not formed on an ideological or philosophical basis (although they may use ideologies for the purpose of rationalization). They are rooted in primeval instincts, anxieties, feelings of distress, and suppressed desires from an earlier period marked by helplessness. In sum, these relations are built on regressive foundations and, therefore, they are imbued with emotions that, if broken loose, may erupt in a way that is beyond control.

The probable growth of regressive relations increases in circumstances of crisis and distress, as we saw in the examples presented earlier. Mischel's[55] distinction between strong and weak psychological situations can help to provide understanding of the psychological conditions that are more likely to engender regressive relations. A strong psychological situation is a structured situation in which people know what is expected of them and how they should behave, a situation in which people feel that there is a large measure of stability and certainty in their lives. The gist of the argument is that the weaker the psychological situation, the more room there is for the emergence of emotional leadership based on projection. In other words, in weak psychological situations, charismatic leadership of all kinds can be a psychological response to the basic human needs for security and certainty. The instinctive longing for a leader in times of crisis was aptly expressed by Eleanor Roosevelt in describing the inauguration ceremony of her husband, Franklin Delano Roosevelt, during a crisis period: "It was quite frightening to hear that when Franklin said in his election speech that he might have to take for himself presidential powers that are generally granted to a president in wartime, just in that part of the speech he got the loudest applause."[56]

A review of the circumstances of the emergence of outstanding charismatic leaders in human history indicates the existence of a recurrent connection between weak psychological situations and the emergence of charismatic leaders. For example, most historians explain the rise of Hitler (who won 38% of the votes democratically) by the state of crisis in Germany between the two World Wars.[57] On this psychological background, Hitler could come and give an emotional answer that resonated in the special emotional circumstances of those days. De Gaulle, a strong authoritative figure in the eyes of the French, responded to the French nation's desire for his return during a period of crisis in Algeria. Khomeini was recalled from exile in France to take over the rule of Iran at the height of the revolution and the collapse of the Shah's kingdom. Lenin, analyzing his success in reaching the status of leader, claimed that it was due largely to his ability to evaluate accurately the critical circumstances of the period, to identify precisely the point at which uncertainty began to grow with the collapse of the Czarist regime and the failure to fill the leadership vacuum, and to inject a measure of stability and order.[58] There is some evidence for all this, but it is not simply a question of leaders emerging in the wake of specific national crises,[59] but of a wide variety of situations, all of which share, at different intensities, the characteristics of a weak psychological situation. For example, various situations of transition are conducive to the emergence of leaders with an emotional effect. Research conducted among veteran combat soldiers in the Israeli army found that many of them clearly remembered their first commanders at the beginning of their military service as leaving the most significant emotional stamp on them in their entire military career. The explanation for this lies in the transition to a different way of life characterized by a great deal of uncertainty, anxiety, and disorientation, which are typical of transition states.[60] The same tendency has been found in more mundane circumstances in organizations. In process-oriented industries (such as petrochemicals) where technological changes are relatively slow and there is a large measure of stability in the production system, processes identified with leadership are conducted in professional teams. On the other hand, industries that manufacture innovative products, in which the groundbreaking aspect is important and there is less routine and stability, are associated more with authoritarian and charismatic figures.[61]

However, although some of the regressive relationships have resonated powerfully in history, mainly due to our inability to understand them in "normal" terms, combined with the destructive drama that often accompanied them (e.g., the case of Hitler), statistically speaking they are rare. Most of the relationships between leaders and followers are not marked by pathological characteristics, certainly not such extreme ones. They contain elements of content, judgment, and sometimes also processes that encourage the development of the followers as individuals. Therefore, we will now look at the nature of this kind of leader-follower relationship, which is the main concern of this book.

LEADERS AND FOLLOWERS: DEVELOPMENTAL RELATIONSHIPS

Freud's metaphor of the leader as a father figure does not necessarily guide the discussion to the existence of unconscious processes relating to parents, as psychoanalytical thinking suggests.[62] Moreover, projection processes are not always regressive in the extreme sense described earlier. Those extreme pathological cases were cited only in order to demonstrate the characteristics and the important implications of intensive regressive relations. However, parental images of leaders, which are mostly presented in the psychoanalytical literature in the context of regression, are not necessarily exclusive to such processes. The image of the leader as parent can also lead to other types of relationships. It is particularly important for the purpose of the present discussion to emphasize the possibility of developmental relations forming between leaders and their people.

In an article summarizing many studies, Popper and Mayseless[63] compared the findings of research on good parenting and good leadership and found great similarity between the two. Both good leaders and good parents were found to be sensitive, responsive, and caring toward their "charges." Both encouraged autonomy, demonstrating a non-judgmental attitude and emotional support. In both cases, the charges were given opportunities to experience development, they received explanations, and nothing was done arbitrarily. In both cases, the parents and the leaders served as examples and were in many senses role models and models for learning and development. Furthermore, in both cases similar results were found. Good parents, like good leaders, succeeded in creating relations of trust with their charges, which strengthened their self confidence and sense of self worth, as well as the wish to achieve more and fulfill more of their potential. It seems, therefore, that despite the potential for dependent relations that is embodied in the asymmetry of parent-child and leader-follower relations (due to the parents' and leaders' greater power and resources), in actual fact this does not necessarily result. This is borne out by considerable research evidence as well as by many theories on parenting relationships.[64] Most parents do not use their superior strength to exploit their children; on the contrary, they see their children's development as one of their major aims, to which they are committed emotionally and morally. The common situation is that parents devote time, energy, and resources to foster their children's emotional and intellectual development so that they will be well equipped for their lives. Almost paradoxically, the greatest achievement of good parents is not their children's dependence on them but precisely the opposite, strengthening their children's belief in their ability to go out and function independently.

This image is relevant to a certain type of relationship between leaders and followers. Positive socialized leaders (those who are not motivated solely by narcissistic deprivation) act in a way designed to empower their followers, namely to build belief in their ability as well as in their intellectual and emotional development. An example of this is the influence of Franklin Delano Roosevelt on millions of Americans when he told them: "The only thing we have to fear is fear itself," and persuaded them to believe in their ability to overcome their difficulties. Moreover, his influence, both in addressing the audience directly and through the parliamentary bodies, led millions of people to believe in their strength to surmount both the economic crisis and the German war machine. Theodore Herzl's major contribution as a leader was the injection of belief into millions of hopeless, downtrodden Jews that they had the strength and the ability to determine their fate. Nelson Mandela not only strengthened the black people's belief in their ability but also by his moral influence (through mechanisms such as the Truth and Reconciliation Commission (TRC)) prevented awful bloody revenge on the whites, revenge that was perceived by many blacks as a natural and more just step.[65]

Developmental relations have this kind of influence in situations both of crisis and of calm (and this distinguishes them from regressive relations, which often emerge as a result of crisis situations). Although there are times and circumstances in which charismatic leadership is more openly manifested, the assumption is that developmental leaders first of all provide a sense of security.[66] In the dynamics of good parenting, the sense of security created by the parents frees the children to occupy themselves with exploration through games, satisfy their curiosity, and engage in activities that are "more developmental."[67] On the other hand, a sense of threat, together with the feeling that there is no one who is "strong and wise" to protect them, will decrease the expressions of initiative, curiosity, and willingness to take risks, and the children's behavior will be focused on achieving a sense of security. Similarly, leaders who provide a sense of security free their people's energies and willingness to engage in more developmental functions, namely to be less preoccupied with their own self and more sensitive and open to others' needs and aspirations.

And what about the needs of the leaders in these relationships? Some developmental theories assert that parenthood is a need. Studies based on attachment theory, for example, show that the infant's need for protection meets with the need of the caregiver (usually the parent) to protect and to give.[68] Leaders not only use parental images in describing themselves and their actions, they also feel that this is their role, or more precisely, they perceive it as their mission. Jim Jones and Charles Manson, as described, felt that the sense of "being fathers" to their people was what prevented them from following their inclination to walk away or commit suicide. Moreover, they testified (as do many parents) that this responsibility gave meaning to their lives. This is the same feeling that inspired Nelson Mandela, Gandhi, and Theodore Herzl, as well as many managers who describe their role and their responsibility. They feel that their involvement, their love and concern, which they often describe using parental images, is the essence of their lives, the cardinal expression of their worth. Some even express the feeling that they are indispensable as "real" parents. But even if many leaders perceive themselves as parents of their followers, there is a difference between the influence of Gandhi and Mandela and that of Jones or Manson. Parenthood, therefore, is not a phenomenon lacking direction and values; it can be good or bad. Leaders whose influence causes the followers "to be more" – more independent, more pro-social, more moral than they were before their encounter with the leader, are close to the models of good parenthood. The important point is that such parents and leaders have a different psychological structure from parents or leaders who create dependence on their parenthood or leadership. The sources and psychological meanings of these differences will be discussed in the chapter dealing with the development of leaders.

Naturally, some situations are more conducive to the occupation with developmental aspects by the very nature of the task. For example, teachers in schools can have considerable influence on their students' emotional and intellectual development. Managers/leaders in research and development organizations, if they do not create suitable conditions for the development of intellectual stimulation, will not succeed in maintaining the degree of innovation, resourcefulness, and creativity required for the development of new processes and products. This is outstandingly the case in military officer and leadership courses, as well as in management courses and schools of business management. Without the conditions that permit developmental experience, together with figures that serve as both incentives and role models, the prospects of development in the direction of independence and competence will decrease.[69]

LEADERS AND FOLLOWERS: SYMBOLIC RELATIONSHIPS

Symbolic leader-follower relations are based on dynamics related to the ideals and aspirations represented by the figure of the leader. When Nelson Mandela was released from jail on February 11, 1990, a mere handful of lawyers and visitors knew the real man. For years large sums had been offered for photographs of him smuggled out of the jail. Most of his exposure was through pictures from his youth, which had been duplicated numerous times. His imminent release was announced a very short time before the actual date, yet thousands came to the jail, crowded round the walls, climbed up trees, and waited for hours. John Battersby, a reporter for the Christian Science Monitor, who waited for him inside the jail, shook hands with him. "I lost all sense of ego," he said, "I saw history and legend merging and becoming reality."[70] Mandela had become, as defined by Nadine Gordimer, "the personification of the future."[71] He had become, as his friends and he himself said, an icon, a symbol. This was so perceptible that some of his friends feared that he would not be able to meet the expectations and that his image would inevitably be dwarfed in the light of these expectations. But Mandela understood perfectly that he was a symbol. All his friends testified that they were amazed by the change in him. He had internalized the fact that he was a symbol, and his deportment became stately and forgiving.[72]

Another historical example of a leader as an emotional symbol is that of Abraham Lincoln. During his lifetime, Lincoln's leadership was extremely controversial. Furthermore, the man who led the war to abolish slavery in the United States, who was identified more than anyone else with values such as equality, this man in his own life accepted social stratification. True, he opposed slavery, but took care to clarify in a letter to a friend: "Naturally I am against slavery, slavery is a bad thing, I have always thought so, always felt so. And yet, in spite of my personal opinion, I do not think that as president I have the right to act officially according to these feelings."[73] In fact, Lincoln only opposed the spread of slavery beyond the states in which it already existed. Furthermore, he thought that slavery had existed in those states before the Constitution was written, and, therefore, it would not be right to infringe on the rights of the slave-owners. In practice, as he expressed in his inauguration speech, Lincoln was more interested in preserving the Union. He became associated symbolically with the war for equality when he published the Emancipation Proclamation, making him the "great emancipator" in historical awareness (though the proclamation only acquired legal status at the end of the war, when Lincoln was no longer alive). Only then did the war acquire an ideological dimension. Historical accuracy thus indicates that the proclamation was formulated at the height of the war. In other words, Lincoln did not go to war to free the slaves, although it was precisely for that cause that he would be accorded symbolic status in the future. Indeed, the "symbolization" of Lincoln provides fascinating evidence of the emotional attitude towards symbols. In an empirical analysis of the process of building Lincoln's leadership in the public awareness, Schwartz[74] describes how Lincoln gradually became a more and more revered leader, a process that began at the beginning of the twentieth century and escalated until 1922, when the large monument was erected in his honor in Washington. By then he was the most revered president of the United States, even more than the founding president, George Washington.[75] The explanations for such processes may be found in theories that ascribe central importance to the human need for meaning.[76] These theories, which are derived from ideas of philosophers, such as John Dewey, Max Weber, John Herbert Mead, and Robert Linton,[77] claim that the need for meaning is a major component in human motivation, hence many of the actions and interactions that people perform stem from the search for meaning. Thus, places and people, as well as certain objects, have expressive emotional meaning. It follows that certain leaders also have expressive meaning. According to this view it was no accident that Lincoln became a powerful emotional symbol in the very period when America went to war in the name of democratic values. It was not by chance that the symbol became magnified when the waves of emigration grew and the question of equal opportunities took central place in the public awareness. It is a fact that many organizations protesting against denial of rights have used the figure of Lincoln to advance their causes. For example, feminist organizations used the civil war and the emancipation of the slaves as an analogy for their struggle, and so did other minorities that felt deprived.[78] History is replete with examples of leaders whose personality, words, and behavior became symbolic representations, representing some transcendental essence beyond the concrete personality of the leader himself. Sometimes such leaders, in their person, their words, and deeds, represent the dream of generations, as in the case of Theodore Herzl. Sometimes they represent the aspirations of a specific period in the history of a certain collective.[79] Thus, David Ben Gurion, who is regarded as the founder and first leader of the State of Israel, in his words, his behavior, his style of dress, his manner, and in the fact of his going as prime minister to live in a kibbutz in the desert, expressed the longing to change the image of the Diaspora Jew into that of a pioneering and fighting figure. All the obituaries for Rabin testify that he has become a symbol (like Lincoln, who became the object of greater admiration after his death than during his lifetime), due to his life story that embodies the image of the Sabra, the new proud Jew, and particularly the warrior, ready to fight for his country. Mahatma Gandhi, in his ascetic behavior and dress, speaking in a local dialect (although he was a lawyer who had acquired his education in England), and in the values he expressed, embodied the spiritual aspect inherent in Indian culture.[80] John Kennedy, who was regarded as one of the most charismatic presidents in the history of the United States, in his outward appearance, his family life, his background, exemplified the American spirit that emphasizes myths of youth, success, wealth, beauty, and individualism. Pierre Eliot Trudeau, who was considered the most charismatic leader in Canadian history (the Canadian press referred to the phenomenon of "Trudeaumania"), in his behavior and attitudes, as well as in the fact of his being both an anglophone and a francophone (he spoke excellent English and French and was, as he used to say, "both Eliot and Pierre"), represented the aspiration of a society of immigrants for integration and a national identity.

Shamir and associates[81] argue that certain leaders, by being the concrete embodiment of a great idea or a broad identity, serve as a psychological means for the enhancement of the followers' self worth. The very fact of their attachment to the leader makes them part of this essence. This was aptly expressed by Macintyre[82] in describing people's attitude toward the leader as towards a story to which they want to belong. That is to say, from the follower's point of view the question is what story does a certain leader convey in his words, his actions, his personal history, and whether "by identifying with that leader do I want to be part of that story?" Turning certain leaders into representatives of cherished ideals, of values that we want to express and share is related to a hierarchy of values. This idea was expressed by sociologist Edward Shils,[83] who distinguished between "center" and "periphery." This refers to a "symbolic center," which certain people are perceived as better able to represent than others. The more they are seen as distinctly representing the symbolic center, the better their chance of being "symbols of leadership," or in Shil's words they have a better chance of being seen as more "charismatic." The flocking of the blacks in America after Martin Luther King reflected a particular population's choice of a person who, in his behavior and words, or in his life story, expressed that population's profound longing. The same is true of Nelson Mandela, whose story and behavior expressed the South African black people's longing for freedom and sovereignty. It is evident that people's aspirations for enhanced self worth are closely related to their society, time, and culture. Leaders with symbolic-emotional influence have to express a relevant and central dimension of a certain social context. Therefore, understanding of a leader's emotional influence involves analysis and understanding of the social and cultural context in which he functions.

The examples cited above presented figures of leaders at the national level. However, symbolic-emotional influence also exists at a more mundane level. A company commander who swears in his soldiers near a national memorial monument at the end of their basic training creates symbolic meaning by binding his soldiers to a tradition relating to the meaning of military service within a broad historical perspective. The commander's "setting an example" is also a symbolic act designed to harness his people's motivation.[84] Even in the business world, which ostensibly operates purely by the rules of profit and loss, there are examples of symbolic leadership. Leaders of large firms such as drug companies emphasize their contribution to the quality and prolongation of life, and leaders of financial organizations take care to emphasize their contribution to society. Common to all these endeavors is the awareness that people wish to see themselves as part of something that is bigger, more principled, and significant than their own immediate material needs.

Leadership in a symbolic perspective may differ from the other two categories of relationship discussed, not only in terms of content but also in the psychological dynamics existing in these relationships. Whereas regressive and developmental relations exist between living people, symbolic relations may also occur with a leader who is not alive. To clarify this point, we can compare it to the attachment people feel to saints. This was described by a historian who studied the process of the formation of saints.[85] "The saint was an escape hatch, a buttress, and a comfort. People appealed to the saint for healing and hope. So great was the need for saints that not only those who were visibly 'holy' were chosen to fill this role. The knowledge of a saint's existence was almost as good as the presence of a real saint. People told miraculous stories about the saints. They attributed to them powers and virtues . . . often, a story was enough to give hope. Scraps of garments worn by the saint (or perhaps not), water that had been touched by the saint (or perhaps not), the saint's blood (or perhaps just red paint), substituted for him. They were imbued with his power, his personality. . ." And what if there was no saint at all whose blood it was, who had worn these garments and blessed this water? Even if there wasn't, it made no difference. "Even if it is based on error, the faith of the believers," writes Cardinal Henriques de Segosio in the thirteenth century, "grants them security.' "[86]

In many cases, if we replace the word "saint" with "charismatic leader" (who is not alive) we will obtain a similar psychological essence. Returning to the general psychological framework that emphasizes the need for a buttress (hidden or overt) to support the leader-follower relations, it may be argued that even when there is no interaction with the leader, the followers' need creates the buttress that supports the "leader within themselves." This idea of relations with a figure inside oneself also appears in psychological approaches such as the object relations approach,[87] but there the internalization is mainly of figures that existed in the individual's personal history (usually the parents). The discussion on symbolic relations extends the repertoire of desires beyond the basic needs of security to needs of social identity or "worthy" meaning. The leader as symbol can represent more clearly ideas that would be abstract and perhaps incomprehensible without this representation by the leader figure. Personification facilitates the believers' identification with ideas and thus often empowers the leader. Leninism, Peronism, Gaullism, and so forth represent worldviews that are identified with them. In this way, the view of leadership relations in symbolic terms differs from the perception of leadership relations from a psychodynamic viewpoint such as object relations.

The discussion on symbolic relations raises another point that is rarely discussed: the use that living leaders make of the figures of past leaders who have become symbols in order to convey their messages and increase their influence. Some leaders who adopted this practice patently understood its powerful psychological effect. Ben Gurion showed that he profoundly understood the symbolic, even mythical power of certain leaders. Referring to the leadership of Lenin after his death, Ben Gurion (who took great interest in Lenin) said: ". . .We see what Lenin was for the party, for all its members and its heads without exception. How he ruled their hearts and minds. How his words, his thoughts, his opinions, were law, an edict that was not to be questioned. How deep was the trust in his understanding and guidance – total and unbounded trust. 'Vladimir Ilich Lenin said so' was the most decisive argument."[88] President Woodrow Wilson made much use of the figure of Lincoln as a symbol of the struggle for values when he was preparing the American nation to participate in the first world war, which he described as a battle for just values. Similarly, black leaders in the United States presented themselves as successors or ideological kin of the leader who charted a dream – Martin Luther King.

The use of such leadership symbols by living leaders may be ascribed to another need, different from those described in the two previous categories – the wish to have an ideological impact. Even if we accept the radical psychological argument that all leaders are motivated by the same desires for power and/or narcissism, we may argue that even if the underlying psychological mechanisms are similar, the sublimations of these leaders are more heroic, more pro-social. Even as sublimations they have great influence. It appears, therefore, that the proximity (constructed in the consciousness of the followers) of living leaders to dead leaders who have become symbols gives the living leaders "charisma points" similar to those attributed to priests, rabbis, or gurus – people who are perceived as related to or the authentic representatives of admired entities or symbols.

In conclusion, the conception of leadership as relationship permits us to understand this phenomenon through the various dynamics between the leader and the followers. The above presentation of the three patterns of relationships is somewhat arbitrary, as the division is not so clear-cut. For example, the perception of a leader as "father of the nation" and the yearning sometimes associated with this may be interpreted in psychoanalytic terms as yearning for an "ancient father," but with the same degree of conviction we can speak of longing for a symbol that represents the "right way" or an idea with which the followers wish to identify. Longing for Ben Gurion or Ataturk may be interpreted as longing for strong and admired figures, namely longing for the stereotype of a protective father, but they can also be interpreted as longing for a simple, pioneering way of life, rooted in ideals, in the case of Ben Gurion, and for western values in the case of Ataturk. Both these types of motives may certainly exist, but if we look at the circumstances of the emergence of the leader-follower relations, the classification proposed here can help us to identify the dominant component in the relationship at a given time. For example, many scholars who have dealt with Hitler's period tend to attribute the Germans' longing for a strong leader to the severe crisis in Germany between the two World Wars. A crisis, according to many scholars, is a psychological basis for regressive relations.[89] Hence, for a more precise method than arbitrary classification we need to look at leader-follower relations in two dimensions: 1) dependence on the leader, and 2) the leader's influence on social and moral values. Leadership relations that cause the followers to have greater belief in their own ability, enhance their value in their own eyes, and also lead to more moral and pro-social thinking that goes beyond the cycle of narcissistic needs or self-interest, are known as **transformational leadership**. In terms of the classification presented here, such leadership is characterized by a lesser extent of exchange relations or regressive processes and a more dominant combination of the characteristics that were described above as developmental and symbolic. The next chapter will discuss transformational leadership and address the question as to what psychological components underlie these leadership relations.

Chapter 4

❧

Transformational Leadership

Many witnesses have described the appearance of Theodor Herzl at the congress in Basle, which laid the foundations for the establishment of a Jewish state.[1] With measured steps Herzl approached the platform, calm and erect, with proud bearing, his black beard, and the unwavering glance shining from his dark velvet eyes; he was greeted by a cheering audience. Amid the resounding cheers, the stamping of feet on the wooden floor, the waving of handkerchiefs and cries of bravo, some bending to kiss his hand, others weeping and hugging each other in joy, Herzl reached the platform but could not begin his speech. Every time he opened his mouth to speak the storm of applause grew even louder. The applause continued for fifteen minutes. The author Ben Ami, overcome by "an irresistible urge," called in a loud voice, "Long live the king!" The call was taken up by many people and reverberated throughout the hall. Herzl gestured impatiently with his hand. In the midst of this commotion, he remained (outwardly) calm. When the cheering finally died down, Herzl delivered his speech, reading from his notes. It was not a rousing speech, but it was marked by a restrained fervor coming from deep inside, something that is always convincing. "We want to lay the foundations for a home which will one day become the home of the Jewish people. This is such a heavy task that we must speak of it only in the simplest words," he began, and then, after describing the situation of the Jewish people in the world, their oppression and humiliation, Herzl concluded by saying, "From ancient times our image has been distorted in the world. The sense of ethnic belonging for which we were so often castigated was in a process of erosion just when we were attacked by anti-Semitism. The anti-Semites strengthened our sense of belonging, we returned home. Zionism is our return to Judaism even before our return to the Land of Israel. . . . We have no intention of giving up in the slightest degree the culture that we have acquired. Rather, we seek to broaden our culture."[2]

When Herzl finished his speech, there was silence, followed by another outburst of cheering. "They cheered him like a king, and people climbed on each others' backs to thank him." Chaos reigned, and in the general excitement chairs and tables were overturned. One of the ladies fainted in the gallery, others waved silk handkerchiefs and cried bravo. Even people who abhorred emotional demonstrations embraced Herzl warmly.[3]

Certain characteristics of this description are not unique or exclusive to Herzl, but recur consistently in descriptions of leaders of the kind described as "charismatic leaders." The hailing of the leader as king, the description of the scene as a regal one, not only point to the tendency for "kingmaking" or even deification of the charismatic leader, they also testify to the force of the suppressed longings that rise to the surface in the meeting with the charismatic leader. We see the waves of blind adoration of an individual who was not known personally to most of those following him so fervently. This manifestation of adoration for Herzl was preceded by rumors and stories, most of them imaginary, which multiplied with the growth of anti-Semitism, which was reaching vast proportions in the west (mainly in France and Austria). It is hard to say how much the people were excited by the man himself and how much they were infected by the excitement of others. Undoubtedly the festive and theatrical nature of the occasion added to the excitement.[4]

Harsh as the comparison may be, destructive charismatic leaders have been described in similar terms. There are numerous descriptions of occasions when Hitler, the charismatic führer, swayed the Germans with his speeches lauding the uniqueness of the German nation. Such speeches were delivered frequently during his campaign to build up the national pride that was so lacking in Germany between the two World Wars.[5] Jim Jones, a leader whose charisma led his people to their deaths in the greatest mass suicide in history, was perceived by his followers (most of whom knew him only from a distance) as a sacred and loving being, whom they described in truly messianic terms.[6]

It appears, therefore, that various types of charismatic leaders arouse extremely powerful feelings in their followers, and that these feelings can blur the distinction between negative charismatic leaders (like Hitler or Jones) and positive ones (like Lincoln or Gandhi). However, a careful analysis beyond the immediate emotional effect indicates important differences.

Herzl himself, the revered "regal" leader, was well aware of some of the meanings of this distinction. For example, looking at the crowd cheering in his honor, shouting "king" and "messiah," he thought: "I saw and heard the birth of a myth. The nation is emotional; the crowds have no clear vision. It seems to me that they have already lost any clear concept of me. A thin cloud is rising around me. Perhaps it will become a pillar of cloud in which I will walk."[7] With his rare gift of seeing himself in a dual perspective, like someone seeing himself in a play within a play, Herzl wrote about this in his diary: "Presumably they would greet a clever impostor with love, just as they greet me, who would not mislead them. Perhaps what I am writing now is the most interesting thing in these journals: how this legend of me was created. As I sat on the platform and listened to the excited speeches and the cheering of my supporters, I resolved in my heart to be always more and more worthy of their trust and love."[8]

This is just how Nelson Mandela thought during the first weeks after his release from jail, as he was borne along on waves of unsurpassed adoration. He avoided using the word "I." He took pains to emphasize over and over again that he was simply the servant of the public. "They can say to me you are 71, you'd better retire, or we don't like your face, please go, and I will obey them."[9] Such attitudes are the essence of the personality difference between positive and negative charismatic leaders. The former are characterized not only by the ability to see themselves in a more balanced perspective, but also by a great sense of responsibility, which makes their leadership a mission on behalf of the people, whereas the latter, as mentioned previously, are motivated by narcissistic deprivation (see the discussion on this in the chapter dealing with the development of leaders). Leadership for them is therefore a route to self-aggrandizement; they seek mainly adoration. The case of Charles Manson, the charismatic and murderous leader of the "Manson family," provides an apt illustration of this pattern (at the pathological level). Incredibly, after the murders, Manson received thousands of letters of support and solidarity. He replied to them: "People need God, God does not need people."[10] Indeed, for some of these leaders, leadership was a real obsession. Death, as in the case of Hitler or Jim Jones, was an alternative to the loss of leadership status that gave them their sole reason for living.[11] The added value of transformational leaders as opposed to "simply" charismatic ones is not only in their more balanced personalities and in what they see as the purpose of their leadership, but also, and perhaps mainly, in the type of emotional effect they have on their followers. In the case of charismatic leaders who are not transformational, the emotional attachment is based on regressive processes. It is, in fact, an encounter between unconscious (sometimes pathological) forces. The attachment to the leader, as described, is primary in the most basic sense. It is a response to distress, or a need that has to be relieved at the psychodynamic level, and then the followers tend to be swallowed up in the figure of the leader and lose their independent judgment. In extreme cases of this type of leadership, the followers in effect become an extension of the leader to the extent that they are unable to function in his absence. Jones' people saw no point in living without him. The attachment to him was symbiotic. When he asked them to take their own lives he said, "I didn't bring you this far to leave you with no future, with nobody to love you, to plan for you and take care of you."[12] His companion, Ann Moore, like all his followers, saw him as the person who made their lives worthwhile. "Jim was the most honest, loving and considerate person I have ever met," she wrote, "he knew how cruel the world is. His love for people is indescribable. Jim Jones showed us that we can live with differences, and we are all human beings. We are going to die because we are not allowed to live in peace."[13] It was the same with Manson whose followers accepted his violent words and behavior unquestioningly. They showed nothing but admiration for him. The first difference (but not the only one, as will be shown later) between leadership that is only charismatic and leadership that is transformational (which also contains a charismatic element) lies in the process known as empowerment, the essence of which is strengthening the followers' beliefs in their own judgment, their ability, and strengths.[14] Whereas non-transformational charismatic leaders weaken their followers by encouraging them to be dependent upon the leader, transformational leaders strengthen their followers' belief in their ability to act autonomously. These differences are significant, among other things, with regard to the range of influence. The influence of charismatic leaders is effective mainly in their presence, whereas transformational leaders can exert powerful influence over a long range; it is internalized by the followers at a level that often persists after the leader has gone, sometimes even over generations. Herzl's great influence caused millions of oppressed, hopeless Jews – who had believed that only an outside force like a messiah could save them – to acquire faith in their own ability to extricate themselves from their downtrodden state. This strength was translated into intensive organizational and political action. Martin Luther King had a similar effect on the black population in the United States. Beyond the ideological arguments, his leadership caused the blacks to believe that their situation was not predetermined and that they had it in their power to change things. The empowerment process, then, means a switch from a state of helplessness or weakness to a state of control of one's life, one's fate, and one's environment. This process is oriented toward change at both the personal and collective level.[15] The empowerment process involves both an internal and an external change. The internal process relates to people's belief in their ability to make decisions and solve their problems. The external change is expressed in the ability to act. Some scholars call the internal change psychological empowerment and the external change political empowerment. According to this distinction, psychological empowerment takes place at the level of consciousness and feelings, whereas political empowerment is a concrete change that enables individuals to take part in decisions concerning their fate.[16]

Psychological empowerment is clearly a precondition for all the external changes, and it has been studied and described extensively in the psychological literature. The major concept in this process, which was first articulated by Albert Bandura, is self efficacy.[17] This refers to cognitive and affective motivational processes related to individuals' belief in their ability to control the events that influence their lives. This belief determines how a person judges his/her situation, and it affects the level of effort, investment, determination, and risk that people summon and maintain in specific tasks. A salient example of empowerment is the psychological influence of Franklin Roosevelt on the American public, which was of major, perhaps critical, importance during World War II.[18] In 1940, when the Germans conquered Europe with lightning speed, the United States was in a very poor state. It was the eighteenth country in the world in terms of military power (below Holland and Switzerland). There were only half a million soldiers in the American army, compared with six million in the armies at the Germans' disposal. Years of economic depression had caused the United States to neglect spending on military development, so that its weapons and technology were outdated. Yet, despite this bleak situation, Roosevelt did not doubt America's ability to win, and, more importantly, he projected this certainty consistently and conspicuously to all around him. Sam Rosenman, one of the people who worked for Roosevelt, describes in his memoirs how the military group around him, including people like George Marshall, Admiral Ernest King, and General Henry Arnold, would leave his office. "I sensed a great calm and a feeling of confidence and determination that reflected the spirit of the man whose office they had just left."[19] But Roosevelt conveyed this feeling beyond the circles in Washington. He switched to a war economy and built hundreds of factories, which caused millions of people to move to the big cities; he formed partnerships between private businesses and government, resulting in the production of airplanes, tanks, military vehicles, machine guns, and ammunition. By 1942, the United States was producing more than the allied countries and was able to supply equipment and ammunition to its allies throughout the world. The question as to how President Roosevelt managed to radiate strength to the entire nation and empower it to such an extent still puzzles many historians.[20] But nobody questions the fact that Roosevelt's leadership was decisive in creating the special atmosphere that spurred a creative endeavor unparalleled in history.

It seems, therefore, that people acquire more strength and belief in themselves as a result of their attachment to a transformational leader and what he represents for them at the psychological or symbolic level. However, contained in the process of empowerment is another process – that of change at the level of motivation. For people (or collectives) to feel sufficiently empowered to act, there must also be motivation to act. Abraham Maslow's motivation theory, probably the most quoted in the psychological literature,[21] refers to a hierarchy of needs. At the bottom of the scale are the survival needs (food and physical safety), and then rising up the scale, the needs for belonging, self esteem, and self actualization. The transformational leader causes his people to rise in their level of motivation as they ascend in this scale.

The primary needs (survival and security) are by their nature common to all living creatures, because they are directly related to biological existence. Because they are primary needs, deprivation at these stages engenders antisocial processes such as segregation or over-attention to details in seeking solutions for their unsatisfied needs. It is a fact that the great Depression in the United States at the end of the 1930s was marked by apathy, introversion, deceit, crime, suicide, and a sense of hopelessness. Burns, for example,[22] points out that manifestations of initiative and what he calls "political behavior" were minimal. The dominant feeling among the American public was "every man for himself." Roosevelt's transformational leadership in his first thirty months of office was directly responsible for delivering millions of Americans from this introverted state. After Roosevelt took office in 1935, industrial workers began to organize for the purpose of negotiating collective wage agreements and collaborating in financial and social initiatives. This was a departure from the traditional American individualism, in the sense that they sought to act for a common goal rather than each one fending for himself. As many have testified, a change occurred in people's motivation, not only to improve their own situation but also to help others, to begin making social changes. Suddenly, many people revealed motivation at the level of the higher needs in Maslow's scale, and this motivation prevailed due to Roosevelt's leadership.

The Jews of Eastern Europe had always been occupied with the attempt to achieve their basic needs of security and survival. The entire history of these populations was a constant endeavor to stay alive in the face of threats from the hostile environment, and to make ends meet. These Jews attempted to keep a low profile so as "not to annoy" the hostile environment. Fear, anxiety, and worry about the future, as well as helplessness and collective apathy toward the environment were the core experience of Jewish life in Eastern Europe. Herzl not only made them want to satisfy the need for belonging in political terms, but actually brought about a change in the structure of their motivation. Testimonies on these Jews' determination and the sacrifices and dangers they were prepared to face under Herzl's influence indicate that for many of them the motivation connected with the need for belonging had become even more important than the needs for physical existence. Certain leaders have had influence on people's motivation to act beyond self interest, to act pro-socially, for the good of society, and even for the fulfillment of universal moral values. President John Kennedy's famous words in his inauguration speech: "Ask not what your country can do for you – ask what you can do for your country"[23] were an appeal to the public to harness their motivation for the general good. Transformational leaders create this kind of effect, this kind of transformation of the followers' motivation. This, in fact, is the most distinct effect that differentiates between transformational leaders and other kinds: the link that they create in their followers' minds between motivation and moral and social values.[24]

The study of ethics and moral behavior has occupied many philosophers since ancient times, but in psychology the work of a few individuals has had decisive influence on the subject. Jean Piaget, who laid the foundations for the study of cognitive development, dealt with moral development in the context of his great work on cognitive development in general.[25] Lawrence Kohlberg developed Piaget's concepts into a theory of moral development, which became the major psychological theory on this subject.[26]

Because of its importance, and because Kohlberg's concepts are relevant to the clarification of transformational leaders' effect on moral behavior, I will briefly summarize Kohlberg's theory here. His major argument is that moral development is related to the ability to understand the meanings of the content. Therefore, the moral development of small children, whose **cognitive** ability is much more limited than that of adults, will be at a lower level. They simply understand less complexity and nuances that have social and moral significance. Based on research conducted by a method he developed, Kohlberg found three main stages of moral development.[27]

A. The pre-conventional stage, in which moral judgments are guided by social reactions – the sanctions that society imposes on those who deviate from the law and the rewards it grants to those who keep the law. Behavior that results in punishment is perceived as bad, and behavior that is rewarded is perceived as good. The moral judgments at this level are characterized by egocentric thinking. At the age of ten, 80% of the moral judgments were found to be on this level, growing less with the rise in age. At age eighteen, only 18% of the judgments are at this level, and the proportion drops to 3% at age twenty-four.[28]

B. The conventional morality stage, in which conformity to social norms is still the basis for moral judgment, but this conformity is no longer motivated by the immediate results of the action, but by the perception that the social order is important in itself and has to be preserved. Thus, judgment at this stage requires the ability to see things from different angles and is expressed in the wish to "do the right thing," to do what is expected or required in order to be seen in a positive light. Such judgments are very rarely found in children aged ten but they become more frequent as the child grows older. At the age of twenty-two, they constitute 90% of the judgments.[29]

C. The post-conventional moral stage, in which individuals no longer accept moral and social imperatives as self evident, but try to define morality in terms of abstract principles and values. The locus of moral judgment shifts to the individual him/herself. At this stage, people are capable of abstraction of the moral values that they choose and of organizing them in a consistent logical frame, according to which they have to act in order to avoid self censure. The individual's private conscience takes central place, and the ability to examine many points of view reaches a very high level of abstraction. Moral judgment at the post-conventional level does not appear at age ten nor at sixteen. By age twenty-four, 10% reach this stage.[30]

Kohlberg's theory, as well as the methods he used, opened a new avenue of research in moral development, the core of which is the attempt to understand moral thinking and argumentation, namely, the way in which people process moral dilemmas in their minds and reach decisions based on thinking, evaluation, and analysis. However, despite the important conceptual contribution of Kohlberg and his followers to the understanding of moral development as a cognitive phenomenon, there still remains the question of motivation to behave morally or pro-socially.[31] Why do people want to act for the good of society, for the general good, for elevated values, sometimes even against their own interests? Why would people want to act "above and beyond," as Bass calls it?[32] This question has occupied scholars in many disciplines, from evolutionists, who see phenomena such as mutual help as an instinct for existential preservation of the reference group,[33] although claims that pro-social and altruistic behaviors are rewarding in the long term, even if this is not evident in the short term,[34] to existentialist philosophical theories,[35] which claim that pro-social behaviors are simply an expression of people's need for meaning.

Martin Hoffman, who has dealt extensively with the empirical aspect of motivation to act morally and pro-socially, asserts that it is a question of distinctly affective processes.[36] The major emotions underlying all motivation to act in such contexts are **empathy** – the ability to enter into the feelings of the other – and **sympathy** – the extension of empathy to the actual wish to help the other. He argues that two basic principles underlie all the social and moral principles: **caring for others**, and **justice**. And these two cannot be realized without empathy and sympathy. There is no need for intricate research in order to find evidence of the validity of this assumption in everyday life. For example, judges (and, in fact, experienced juridical systems) know well that jury members' feelings of empathy and sympathy have considerable influence on the evaluation of morality.[37] Perhaps this can be seen more clearly if we look at the opposite end of the continuum – the absence of empathy and sympathy. History is replete with examples in which the dehumanization of the "other" (which is a form of brainwashing to eliminate empathy and sympathy) led nations to violence, revenge, and destruction. There is evidence, some of it horrifying, of how prisoners of war cruelly attacked their friends after being stripped of feelings of empathy by brainwashing or other methods.[38] Many leaders in history have created this effect. The most outstanding example is clearly the Nazi regime's delegitimization, dehumanization, and demonization of the Jews, which enabled the Germans to abuse Jews much more cruelly (and some say eagerly) than they did others.[39]

However, there are also quite a few examples of leaders whose influence on their followers has enhanced their capacity for empathy and sympathy and thus engendered a transformative social and moral effect. Nelson Mandela, referring to the thousands of victims and their families who were interrogated and tortured by the police of the de Klerk and Botha regime, stated that apart from Hitler's genocide of the Jews, no such severe crimes had been committed in human history as those committed by the South African governments against their black populations. Yet despite this feeling, which was shared by all the members of resistance movements in South Africa, Mandela repeatedly argued that "there is a need for understanding and not for revenge, there is a need to redress the wrongs but not for acts of retaliation, there is no need to make victims."[40] "And above all," he insisted (using an argument that became a major theme in his approach), "we can forgive but we cannot forget."[41] The concrete expression of this attitude was the establishment of the Truth and Reconciliation Commission (TRC) headed by Archbishop Desmond Tutu. The very purpose of the commission was not to forget. As well as creating a psychological mechanism that both gave a sense of justice and tempered the desire for revenge, it set in motion a process that emphasized the future rather than remaining trapped in the past (while still keeping alive the memory of the past). The initiators of this mechanism had really learned from history. They wanted to avoid a situation similar to the Nuremberg trials of the Nazis, which could turn people into martyrs and saints. Therefore, they examined other models that had been applied in Eastern Europe and in South America, and found this solution, which was defined as the happy medium between "amnesty and amnesia."

This was not an easy solution for many of those who had struggled against the regime; they were filled with a burning desire for revenge. "I know that my wife's murderers will go free" was the angry response of Joe Slovo, one of the resistance leaders, and many felt the same. Nevertheless Gillian, Slovo's daughter, expressed the more moderate attitude that Mandela had managed to instill into the majority: "The TRC is not supposed to do absolute justice, it is supposed mainly to expose the truth."[42]

Despite the harsh criticism of Mandela, which became even harsher when the findings of the commission were published, Mandela was totally confident that he was right. Furthermore, he stubbornly insisted on being optimistic and seeing the good in human nature. He regarded this as a human and political message and demonstrated it in his own behavior. He did not bear a grudge against his jailers for the decades of his imprisonment. He met with them without trying to settle old scores. He did not take revenge either on de Klerk or on Botha, but treated those heads of the apartheid regime generously and forgivingly. Mandela's transformational contribution was aptly summarized by Graca Machel, who was closer to him than anyone else during that period: "Mandela symbolized forgiveness, understanding and the willingness to solve problems with a view to the future. If he had come out of jail and transmitted other messages, I can promise you that this country would have gone up in flames."[43]

Gandhi demonstrated his transformational political approach in a landmark case known as the "tax revolt" against the heavy taxes imposed by the British on farmers in the Bombay region. Gandhi led the struggle against the British. The farmers did not pay the taxes, the British arrested thousands, but money was sent from all corners of the country to help the peasants in their struggle. Within a short time negotiations were held and a compromise was reached, reducing the tax from 22% to 5%. This struggle, noted Gandhi in his diary, became a message illustrating the use of "passive resistance" against the British.[44] This form of non-violent struggle was used again in March 1930, in a campaign Gandhi led against the taxes on salt, taxes in the range of £8,000,000 levied by the British Empire, mainly from the poor. The sight of the sixty-year-old Gandhi dressed in a white robe marching at the head of thousands, making speeches, praying, but preventing violence, became a symbol of the form of struggle he introduced and acted as a political lever. We see here a rare case in history where consistently moral behavior became a powerful political force embodied in the person of one man, who was more like a monk than the stereotypical figure of a leader transmitting power and aggression.

However, the examples cited here may give the impression that transformational leadership can exist only on a national level. Indeed, as shown by Shamir,[45] it is easier to "magnify" national figures, it is easier to ascribe romantic, larger-than-life images to people who are associated in our awareness with historic events such as nation-building, constituting a national identity, and similar dramatic milestones in the life of the collective. But transformational leaders do not exist only at these levels, although they are much more visible at the top (for reasons mentioned in the introduction). Therefore, we will now examine transformational leadership in less dramatic contexts. Leadership that may be called "transformational leadership in everyday life" is a phenomenon that we often encounter in all spheres of life.

TRANSFORMATIONAL LEADERSHIP
IN EVERYDAY LIFE

When Gary Convis was appointed vice president of manufacturing at New United Motor Manufacturing (NUMMI) in California, he was told by NUMMI president, Ken Hayashi: "I want you to run production as if you had no power at all. Everyone in the plant knows you are the vice president of manufacturing. Your everyday ability to listen, to guide, to reach a consensus around the key issues is what you will be evaluated on more than anything else."[46] Thus, perhaps unwittingly, Hayashi gave Convis a lesson in transformational leadership, namely, how to influence people, how to get them to do more and be more without coercion or threats of force. The entire history of NUMMI is a striking example of transformational leadership in everyday life (which occurred in the almost optimal conditions of a laboratory experiment). In 1963 a production plant of General Motors was opened in Freemont, California. The decision to establish it there was the result of the growth of the motor market on the west coast.

In 1978, the plant employed 7,200 workers and in 1982 it simply closed down. "Those were years of war,"[47] thus one of the foremen described the relations between the management and staff, who were unionized. The atmosphere was described as one of "violent suspicion." Everything had to be signed and documented; every achievement of management or workers was gained by aggressive confrontations. And thus, in a climate of strikes and confrontations, with countless production problems, they somehow managed to keep the plant going for years, until finally, in 1982, after one of the strikes, the GM central management decided it had had enough and closed it down. One year later, in 1983, the plant was reopened under the joint ownership of Toyota and GM, and headed by a Japanese management team. In 1988, the plant won the national prize for excellence. It manufactured eighty-seven cars per day (compared with Buick's fifty). The plant in Freemont, California became GM's most efficient factory. Cynics can, of course, argue that the actual closing and reopening of the plant were enough to create pressure leading to improvement, but this argument is not valid in view of the fact that a similar plant, in Van Nuys, California, was closed down and reopened in almost identical circumstances, and after a while it was closed down permanently because it failed to function properly.[48] Furthermore, the employees' involvement and contributions were much greater by any standard. On average, 3.2 efficiency optimization proposals per worker were submitted, and 81% of the proposals were accepted. When 86% of the staff suggest efficiency optimization proposals, this is an unmistakable sign of alertness and involvement. The interesting and unique point in this case is that the employees were the same people who had worked in the plant in its previous version. They were not offered a more generous pay package. They were still unionized. In fact, nothing in the structural sense had changed substantially. What had changed, and dramatically so, was the way the people were managed. The company shifted from the old traditional ways of operating, based on formal authority and power, to a style of operation through leadership – by influencing people's feelings and thus harnessing their motivation to act "above and beyond." The analysis of this case indicates certain directions in the leadership that bear psychological significance. For example, it was made clear in advance that firing would not be used as a method or a threat in the relations between management and staff. Such an attitude, in Maslow's terms, ensures that people's attention, psychological energies, or motivations will not be focused on questions of survival and security (which are guaranteed), but on the higher levels in Maslow's hierarchy, relating to needs for belonging, self esteem, and finally self actualization. This is manifested in the growth in personal involvement, in the ideas and creativity that people express, and in the level of trust they demonstrate towards the management and work teams. Considerable efforts are devoted to coaching, training, and development of the workers. Toyota brought over 400 instructors from Japan, sent 600 employees to Japan to learn, and in addition, all the employees receive training in which they internalize thoroughly not only the production method but also the philosophy, whose essence is trust and respect. This case illustrates how a transformation was effected in the workers' motivation, not in heroic circumstances or complex tasks requiring great knowledge and skills, but in a labor-intensive industrial plant where the work processes are mostly standardized.[49] There is no clearer demonstration of the argument that companies can reach outstanding achievements with quite ordinary people.[50]

Similarly, empowerment is not necessarily a process that characterizes elite organizations or exceptional people. This was demonstrated in the case of AES (Applied Energy Services), a company founded in 1981 by Roger Sant and Dennis Bakke, two people who had worked in public service in the field of energy and decided to found a company "that works differently." They wanted to raise $3,000,000 in order to establish their company, but managed to raise only 1.3 million (incidentally, amazing evidence of the company's success is the fact that an investment of $10,000 in foundation stocks in 1982 yielded $20,000,000 in 1999). There is a wealth of evidence on the success of the firm according to every known parameter. Just for the sake of comparison with other organizations in the same market, in 1999 the return for investment was 178% higher than the average in this industry (energy), and the profit was 203% higher than the average profit. In the past five years there was a growth of 41% in profits. The return to stockholders was 531%, which was an astronomical growth considering the fact that this is not an Internet or computer firm or a company that has invented some new product.[51] An analysis of this firm's story, its functioning and development, clearly indicates the founders' transformational leadership as the explanation for its success. More specifically, the two founders aimed to set up a company that would be the opposite of the public organization that they knew so well; they wanted a company that was not bureaucratic and was based on maximal decentralization. In fact, the founders did not regard themselves as managers in the usual sense; they saw themselves as shaping values and a spirit in which people could act freely. One expression of this is the structure of the company: it has no headquarters, there are no human resources, there is no conventional hierarchy. A few people at the center serve mainly as a source of information and advice for the company sites scattered around the world, which are run autonomously. Four major values underlie the empowering atmosphere of the company: 1) fun, 2) fairness,

3) integrity, and 4) social responsibility. The management praxes are derived from these values; otherwise, as the founders say, "it's just technique and talk."[52] These values are expressed in aspects such as choice of staff or a wage policy that grants bonuses in three areas: individual work, teamwork, and the work of the entire plant. The wage policy thus reflects the values of fairness and integrity, encourages teamwork, and stimulates the people to look at the whole picture. Both in the choice of people and in the ongoing activities, great emphasis is placed on enjoying the work and taking initiative. The atmosphere encourages the staff to take responsibility, to initiate without being afraid of making mistakes, not to fear taking risks. This kind of atmosphere attracts people who want responsibility and scope for action, want to be empowered. And the fact is that two thirds of the employees came from other firms in the energy industry, which paid higher salaries but gave them no freedom of action and paid little attention to the value of enjoying one's work.[53] The story of Ralph Stayer,[54] manager of a sausage-manufacturing firm in Johnsonville, became famous as a case exemplifying transformational leadership in everyday life and is studied in prestigious schools of management. Here again, we see a company that is labor-intensive (unlike decentralized high-tech industries, which depend on experts), and as such, characterized by standardization of work processes – factors that usually create centralized organizational structures and a clear division between management and a dominant professional team on one side, and workers, who generally perform standard tasks on the other.[55] Despite the success of the company, Ralph Stayer wanted to realize his vision, which was more ambitious than the financial management of a sausage factory. He saw in the company an opportunity to conduct a social economic experiment that would prove his claim that people by their nature want to excel, want to find an outlet for their personal abilities, in contrast to the assumption prevailing in some organizations (not always on the conscious level, and certainly not spoken out loud) that people are lazy by nature, tend to do the necessary minimum, and in fact will not work properly without supervision and the fear of sanctions.[56] Stayer introduced almost total decentralization at the structural level, and intensive processes of empowerment at the psychological level. As in the case of AES (which is a more technologically sophisticated company), the workers were divided into work teams and given full authority to screen and select new employees without any intervention from management. "After all," said Stayer, "they, the teams, are going to work with the new people, obviously they will know better than anyone else who is suitable for them." Moreover, they received budgetary powers with transparency of the data, so that they also had the authority to set salaries. In addition, bonuses were based not on output

but on development. For example, people who took courses in inventory management, team management, and the like, received bonuses. This fostered a norm of learning and development, responsibility, and involvement. In fact, said Ralph Stayer, "my role is confined to the philosophical level (setting basic assumptions) and determining the ultimate standards of the product, all the rest is managed by the workers." And he added, "the most amazing thing is to see the people's enthusiasm (the same people who had previously worked in the company and by their own testimony thought that Ralph Stayer had gone out of his mind when he came with his new ideas). This is my greatest satisfaction, to see people enjoying their work, it brings out the best in them."[57] A thought provoking indication is the fact that the firm, which had been successful prior to this experiment, became a spectacular financial success through application of these principles. In general, the literature on organizations contains numerous examples of transformations generated by leaders. Thomas Watson Sr. brought about a dramatic transformation in the thinking, operation, and management in IBM; Robert Hutchins turned the mediocre Chicago University into a leading academic center. One could point to many such examples, showing how things looked before the arrival of the leader and how they looked afterwards.[58] These transformations occurred first of all in the hearts and minds of the organization members, and the more they were internalized the more long-lasting were the transforming effects, becoming part of the organization's "genetic code."[59]

We don't need to go to outstanding and booming industries to see transformational leadership in action. Such leadership also appears in more mundane contexts, for example in the field of education. Take the story of Jaime Escalante, a Hispanic math teacher who worked in a Los Angeles suburb.[60] Escalante taught at an under-achieving school with students who came from families living in slums ridden with drugs and violence, and saw themselves as lacking any chance of reaching higher education (and therefore lacked motivation). He led these students to meaningful achievements, to outstanding success in examinations in which only 2% of the students in the United States succeed, examinations that are a condition for admission to prestigious colleges like Princeton, Harvard, and Yale. The success was so spectacular that the authorities suspected cheating, and the students were forced to take the exams again under the supervision of the federal authorities. The second time around, their results were even better. For example, from Escalante's first class (1982), fifteen of the eighteen students he taught (all Hispanic) were admitted to college, a proportion well above the average in the Hispanic community. (A follow-up report in 1987 revealed that nine of these were studying for a second degree.) Escalante's influence on the students, and hence on their achievements, was so outstanding that he was awarded a special medal by President Ronald Reagan. When the students described the sequence of events that brought them to such high levels of achievement, it emerged that the teacher's main influence was in motivating the students and making them feel that they could do it, that they were capable of learning and succeeding. He would get up early and go to the school early to meet and teach children who also came earlier (because he had asked them and he was prepared to do so). He would invite students to his home and teach them mathematics over a meal. He visited the homes of absentees. In short, he became a kind of father, caring and concerned for them while demanding hard work and discipline – he became a transformational leader. There is a great deal of research evidence on the immense motivational power of expectations consistently transmitted by leaders in various spheres (particularly through their behaviors).[61] In certain circumstances, these expectations often become "self fulfilling prophecies." For example, Rosenthal and Jacobson,[62] in a well-known experiment, presented a sample of teachers with false information about their students, saying that some of them had been found in tests to have "high learning potential" and were likely to make great progress in their studies. Other students were not given any special grade by the researchers. In fact, no such tests of learning ability had been done, and the students who were described as having "high learning potential" were chosen **at random**. The data collected at the end of the school year showed that the students who had been marked as having "high learning potential" achieved higher grades than their classmates who had not been so marked. When the more successful students were questioned in an attempt to understand what had happened, they reported that they had been treated in a way that raised their motivation and their belief in their own ability (which also strengthened their motivation to work hard). They were encouraged, they were given feedback, made to feel that they were good; briefly, they were made to want to make endeavors "above and beyond" – a classic effect of transformational leadership. Thus, teachers, and perhaps especially teachers, can be transformational leaders.[63]

It seems that at all levels – political, organizational, educational, social, or family – the essence of transformational influence is in the clear messages emanating from a deep inner sense of knowledge of the "right thing," of knowing the way. Herzl not only believed almost obsessively that a Jewish state was the only possible solution for anti-Semitism, he also believed with all his heart that the European countries would agree and even be happy with this solution of the problem of the Jews living among them.[64] Nelson Mandela often used the metaphor of the rainbow to describe a future society tolerant of all colors. He knew very well where he wanted to lead South African society.[65] Gandhi's clear messages regarding the goal and the path to reach it derived from a coherent worldview.[66] Walt Disney, from his early youth, was determined to create "the biggest theater in the world," in which parents and children could have fun together.[67] The Hispanic teacher Escalante knew exactly what he wanted to achieve with his students, but beyond that, he knew what message he wanted to convey to the American environment in which he and his students lived.[68] Yanush Korchak, the famous educator who went to the Nazi death camp together with his wards in the children's home, had a clear educational conception regarding the nature of children and the right way to educate them.[69]

Different terms have been used to express this sense of knowing the way: vision, message, dream, and conception. All of these are important and essential, but they cannot become transformative leadership action if they are not manifested in behavior. Consistent determined behavior, inspiring enthusiasm and trust, is what transmits the leader's messages, and without it they are merely words, pamphlets, position papers, meaningless hollow posters.

For nine years, from the time he conceived his vision (following the Dreyfus Affair) until his death at the age of forty-four, Herzl was driven, like an engine running non-stop, by belief in his vision. He lived at a dizzying pace, slept very little, suffered excruciating pain and heart attacks. His private life was unbearable, many people attacked or mocked him, few were on his side, certainly at the beginning, but he was determined. His belief in the possibility of a different and better future was the source of the immense energy that he devoted that, in less than ten years, left its mark on millions for generations to come. Similarly, it was only deep inner conviction of the rightness of his path that gave Nelson Mandela the strength to enter jail as a young man and emerge after twenty-seven years at the age of seventy-one, not a broken man but rather, full of faith in a better and brighter future. Gandhi was imprisoned, beaten, his ashram in Ahmedabad was threatened with closure, yet despite all this he did not give up, did not compromise, and became the symbol of a way of life and behavior that reflected his fundamental moral conception.

Many people did not believe in Walt Disney's vision; technical experts did not believe it was possible to create musical animation, cinema people did not believe it was possible to create movies in color. Even his brother, his business partner, often thought it was a waste of money, nevertheless Walt Disney pursued his vision until he succeeded in infecting many people with his enthusiasm. Dennis Bakke and Roger Sant, heads of AES, like Ralph Stayer, manager of the sausage factory in Johnsonville, did not hang posters about empowerment in the corridors of their plants. They expressed their views in resolute and unequivocal actions, reflected in the wage policy, the bonus policy, the delegation of authority, methods of supervision, methods of recruitment and placement; in short, all the practices of everyday management conveyed messages of empowerment. Escalante came to teach in one of the worst schools in Los Angeles, which functioned in a delinquent environment. He was the target of mockery by boys and girls who hated everything connected with the establishment and were tired of teachers who came and left disappointed. Escalante's great success in the students' achievements, and more important, in their self concept, was not brought about by saying nice words to them. These children were suspicious to start with, and were often absent from school. Moreover, the social world and status system that was significant to them was outside the school, outside the "orderly world," in the life of the neighborhood gangs. Escalante succeeded in transforming them because he never gave up on a child who dropped out. He simply went to the child's house to bring him/her back; he went to meet with the children in the gang's hangout. He demanded of his students to study more, and arrived earlier to be with them whenever they needed him, he devoted hours on end, beyond his working hours, teaching, persuading, encouraging, and supporting them. In fact, he was a workaholic. Yanush Korchak, a physician who turned out to be a famous educator known for gaining enormous achievements, devoted himself wholly to education. He had lived with the children in the home, and he stayed with them even when they were taken by the Nazis to the concentration camps to be executed. Although he could have escaped this fate, he preferred to die with them. He knew each child individually and was both a father and mother to them and a role model. Ben Gurion's motivational influence did not stem from his rhetorical speeches but from his lifestyle and his behavior. When he spoke of making the desert bloom, he gave substance to his words by going himself to live in a kibbutz in the desert.

It seems, therefore, that this combination of a message that stems from deep inner conviction and its concrete expression reflected in consistent behaviors is what creates the spirit, that psychological sensation known as esprit de corps, which causes people to do their best. A point worthy of emphasis is that the vision first sustains the leader himself. I often compare this to the obsessive urge of artists and writers who have works of art inside themselves, charging them with energy, enthusiasm, and endless tenacity. If the leader's vision comes from this inner fire, it is spread most convincingly to those around him in ever widening circles, as the evidence indicates. When leaders technically adopt a vision of others, or construct (usually with the help of external advisors) visions that do not express real inner passion, they do not succeed in convincing anyone. Thus, Benjamin Disraeli's maxim "Man is only truly great when he acts from his passions" has a strong psychological basis, and people discern this clearly. Psychology researchers have attempted empirical examinations of the meanings and expressions of transformational leadership. The first and best known of these researchers, Bernard Bass,[70] conducted studies that presented the typical behaviors of transformational leaders. Before starting to construct instruments to measure such behaviors, he conducted a pilot study in which seventy senior managers were asked to describe a transformational leader whom they had met in the course of their lives. A transformational leader was described as someone who had raised their consciousness and expectations for achievements, influenced them in moving to higher needs, and caused them to work harder for aims broader than simple self interest. All the respondents stated that they knew at least one person who matched this description, and when they described this person's influence on them, they said, for example, that s/he had caused them to work without thinking of financial reward; they spoke of their wish to come up to the leader's expectations. Some of them said that the leader had caused them to be more emotionally committed to an organization or a task; others said that they simply wanted to imitate the leader. Many used images such as "a kind father" or "a benevolent father" who served them as a model of integrity and fairness. The leader's demand for high standards of performance from his people was accompanied by emotional support, advice, appreciation of their endeavors and achievements, and openness. He gave his people a sense of security along with a sense that he was paying close attention. He allowed them a high degree of autonomy and encouraged their independent development. Furthermore, he was willing to share his knowledge and experience with them. The key words that recurred in most of the descriptions were "trust," "strong liking," and "respect."[71]

The answers that were received in the pilot study were analyzed and served as a basis for the development of a questionnaire permitting a greater degree of statistical generalization.[72] The questionnaire used a statistical method known as factor analysis.[73] In the preliminary analysis three factors of transformational leadership were found: 1) charisma (which at a later stage was divided into "idealized influence" and "inspirational motivation," for conceptual reasons and also for the purpose of a more focused statistical analysis; 2) individualized consideration, and 3) intellectual stimulation. These will be described later.

Charisma – some typical behaviors of the charisma factor were: "He (the leader) makes the people around him enthusiastic," "Excites me with his vision that we are expected to/can realize," "Enhances my optimism regarding the future", "Gives me a sense of purpose." This factor in its first version comprised eighteen items that accounted for 66% of the variance. This finding supports the argument that transformational leadership is in the end an emotional phenomenon.

We can see that the emotions associated with the charisma factor are mainly faith in the leader, pride (one of the items is "I am proud to be associated with the leader"), the sense of a goal and meaning. Clearly, such feelings may also arise towards charismatic leaders who are not necessarily transformational. It is well known that similar emotions were felt towards Jim Jones, Charles Manson, and Benito Mussolini, all charismatic leaders in the eyes of their followers, who had faith in them, believed in their vision (although it was destructive, they did not see it that way), and were proud to be their followers. Thus, the charisma factor, although it is central in creating the emotional foundation for the relations with the leader, is not sufficient in itself to bring about the psychological and conceptual transformation described. Such a transformation is effected by the dynamic mixture with the other two factors: individualized consideration and intellectual stimulation. Only this composition, this gestalt (which is more than the simple addition of the factors) creates the transformational effect. Moreover, the emotions toward the transformational leader are generally formed differently from those felt toward an actor or a singer, for example. As described by leadership scholar Hollander,[74] in most cases these feelings are not formed all at once but grow over a long period, as the leaders accumulate what Hollander calls idiosyncratic credit in their followers' eyes. The image "idiosyncratic credit" is taken from the world of banking, where a person receives credit after proving that he is worthy of it over a long period. As described at the beginning of this book, an analysis of many transformational leaders indicates that most of them were not marked by external characteristics such as good looks or eloquence, which are often attributed to the popular idea of charisma. The charismatic relations grew out of long psychological processes. The story of Moses in the desert can serve as a symbolic example. His path as a leader was not smooth; he constantly met with resistance and suspicion on the part of his people, it took a long time and severe tests for trust to grow in his ability to lead. Truman's "charisma" was non-existent at the start, nor was it born when he entered upon his role as president of the United States. It was built up over a long series of decisions and actions, as his credit grew. Gandhi was far from being a charismatic figure in the usual associative sense of a leader who sweeps his people along with him. He was unimpressive in his outward appearance. He became a "charismatic legend" after a long process during which his image was constructed. The question of social distance[75] is also significant in building the emotions that underlie charismatic relations. As described in the previous chapter, when leaders are distant their psychological credit is built on the basis of images, "cognitive clues," projections, and so forth, whereas when the leader is close, emotions develop on the basis of consistent behavior patterns. As mentioned, every combat officer knows very well that setting a personal example has more motive force than external appearance or ardent speeches. Parents' behavior patterns influence their children more than any other source of influence.[76]

For these reasons, the hundreds of studies that have been conducted on charismatic and transformational leaders in organizations have focused on the leaders' **behaviors**.[77] This angle of analysis brings us back to the argument that it is necessary to distinguish between political leadership and leadership in other contexts. One of the important distinctions is, as described, the manner of building trust and the weight of the leader's behavior in this process.

Intellectual Stimulation – the essence of this factor is the atmosphere created by the leader and the conditions that enable the people around him to think in new, creative, and diverse ways. Examples of items that appear in this factor are: "He causes people to look at problems from different angles," or "He seeks different points of view in solving problems."[78] We see here that the effect of a transformational leader in this field is the reverse of the well-known words of Walter Lipman: "If we all think alike, then none of us thinks very much." However, it is not a question simply of the intellectual aspect; the important things are openness, tolerance, willingness to listen to others, and above all, the ability to accept the idea that there may be points that the leader has not thought of. The dark side of this factor is the leader's "ego size" – a variable that, according to historical evidence, has been the downfall of many leaders who appeared to have all the skills and talents to become great leaders. There are many examples, at all levels of leadership, of phenomena such as "framing" – where one is bound to a certain conception without examining other possibilities or assumptions (the opposite of intellectual stimulation), often due to obtuseness, arrogance, lack of openness. This, apparently, was what caused Watson Jr., head of the "blue giant" – IBM – to miss the personal computer market. The great transformational leaders (some of whom have been mentioned in this book) not only made room for the ideas and thoughts of others, they initiated processes that gave maximal expression to the factor of intellectual stimulation. In Herman Wouk's well-known novel, *Winds of War,* one of the characters is a young naval officer who corresponds with

President Roosevelt from various places where he serves. Every time he goes to Washington on leave, Roosevelt invites him for a chat and listens to him attentively. This example, even if fictitious, characterizes the spirit of Roosevelt. He not only listened to those who came to him, he strove to meet with people from all walks of life and all social classes. He wanted to listen to them, to sense the mood directly, he initiated processes of intellectual stimulation: testing basic assumptions and examining as many different points of view as possible.[79] This example illustrates another aspect that was mentioned earlier, but will be emphasized again. Intellectual stimulation does not mean that the leader has the greatest intellect, as many tend to think. This is not the point at all, the greatness of transformational leaders is that they do not compete with or envy people more intellectual than themselves, nor do they toady to them. Truman respected George Marshall's intellect and listened to him without envy or power struggles, but (as will be shown subsequently) he did not belittle himself and was capable of deciding contrary to the opinion of the man he valued so highly. In contrast, Woodrow Wilson, professor and president of Princeton University, an intellectual who became president of the United States during World War I, was not successful in creating intellectual stimulation. It is doubtful whether he was capable of stimulating others to think differently, particularly in a critical manner.[80]

In everyday life this factor has differential weight, largely contingent on the circumstances of the action. Clearly, in organizations or tasks that are highly standardized there is less importance to processes of intellectual stimulation. But this factor is of great importance in research and development industries, for example, where creative thinking, new ideas, and original perspectives may be crucial to the survival of these systems. It is also extremely important in the sphere of education, including education in the home.

Individualized Consideration – this factor relates to developmental processes that are described in terms such as "empowerment." Examples of items that appeared in this factor were: "He (the leader) devotes time to training and coaching," or "He helps (his workers/his people) to develop their strong sides." A comparison with behaviors identified in studies on good parenting found great similarity between the behaviors of good parents and of transformational leaders. For example, like transformational leaders (particularly in organizations), good parents encourage their people/children to take part in setting goals that are high but attainable. This combination both develops achievement orientation and allows for the accumulation of experiences of success – which is the most meaningful input in building self efficacy (this variable will be elaborated upon with the help of examples in the next chapter). Furthermore, both good parents and transformational leaders provide feedback on performance, instrumental assistance, and above all, emotional support of the type that promotes autonomy and courage. They are also the source of those psychological strengths that are always needed but are vital in times of crisis (as we will see from the biography of outstanding transformational leaders in the next chapter).

Although an overview of the factors of transformational leadership shows that the weight of the factors that are not included in "charisma" is statistically lower, a scrutiny of the contents of these other factors and the psychological essence that they express indicates that they are decisive in determining the direction of the leadership, especially in the case of transformational leadership in everyday life. Without these factors, leadership can be a value-less psychological phenomenon. A leader may be able to excite and inflame people, manipulate their feelings in various directions, not all of them meaningful on the personal or social level, some of them extremely destructive. It is the presence of the other aspects beyond charisma that makes the leadership phenomenon positive, creative, leading to achievements and development, and sometimes even noble. It can, as research has shown, bring out the best in the followers and the leaders.

In conclusion, the discussion on transformational leaders reveals a broad range of behaviors in terms of style, manner of speech, and naturally, the conditions under which they operated. The folksy Mandela displayed different behaviors from those of Herzl, who was more distant and even perceived as "regal" (some thought him arrogant).[81] Ben Gurion's ornate style of speech was different from the simple, direct, and intimate style used by Franklin Roosevelt in his "fireside chats." But when the discussion turns to the motivation and expectations of leaders and followers, the descriptions become more similar. It appears that although the methods or the style of speech and action differ, the essence is the same. Hence, it is necessary to look beyond the level of concrete behaviors at a specific point in time. Common to all transformational leaders, whatever their style, is that they touch (perhaps not always consciously) the good in people. Their basic action consists of tapping the positive strengths of their people. Here we come to the question of basic assumptions[82] regarding human nature, assumptions that underlie the development of the various theories. "Human nature is fundamentally good/bad" is an example of a possible basic assumption, which finds various expressions in psychological thinking, from Freudian psychology, which tends to determinism and a certain degree of pessimism, to what is known today as "positive psychology,"[83] which is rooted in the assumption that people aspire to the good. This issue appears to be beyond empirical proof (one can bring evidence to support both views of human nature). It is doubtful whether some of the transformational leaders gave much thought to these questions, but there is no doubt that their influence was oriented towards positive aspects, as proved by the fact that the transformations they brought about were in positive directions. The very existence of such influences, the existence of examples like those cited here, indicates that a dichotomous view of basic assumptions regarding human nature is too simplistic, because there are also some extremely harsh and cruel examples of the influence of leaders. Perhaps both themes exist, and the uniqueness of transformational leaders lies in their ability to evoke and harness the positive forces. This brings us to the possibility that these are **learned** behaviors. It is a fact that phylogenetically inferior animals, which appear to be mainly occupied with the needs of survival and the territorial imperative do not necessarily behave according to the dynamics of winner/loser or instant gratification of needs. France de Waal,[84] who studied animal behaviors, found manifestations of behavior that cannot be explained by the deterministic logic of self interest and instant gratification. There is research evidence from as far back as ancient Greece that whales will not abandon a wounded friend even at the cost of risking their own lives. They will shelter a wounded fellow-whale from a fishing boat with their own bodies. This fact is so well-known that whale hunters exploit it for their own purposes. As soon as the whale hunter sights a school of whales he only has to injure one of them to ensure that the other members of the school will swim around the boat. How can we explain the warning cry of a bird that enables others to escape the claws of a predator while drawing attention to itself? Or dolphins that support a wounded companion close to the surface of the water in order to prevent it drowning? There appears to be some kind of "learned legacy," dictating codes of behavior that cannot be explained by existing short-term paradigms. Studies based on one of the major experimental paradigms in social psychology, known as "the prisoner's dilemma," demonstrate that there are aspects such as trust that can be learned or acquired over time – a genuine process of building credit. For example, two psychologists[85] who translated the "prisoner's dilemma" to a simulation game in which it is possible to lose and win money, showed that the players revealed a growing tendency to cooperate when they played again with the same players. The reason is simple. When the game is played several times, a player who gets to know the other players more intimately is later prepared (and might even be happy) to cooperate with his friends. Moreover, when they trust each other the players discover in the course of the repeated games that they can all benefit from the game by playing cooperatively. In this way, they can reduce to a minimum the possibility of loss. Here we see in an experiment an illustration of the great profit for both sides that is only possible in conditions of trust. The experiment reveals a process of learning leading to a change in behavior from the beginning, when the considerations of each player did not include others, to a cooperative strategy that channeled the tendencies for optimization both of the general good and the good of the individual. This, as stated, is an analysis based solely on interests. However, as described throughout the book, people are not motivated solely by instrumental motives but are also stimulated by other, expressive, motives. Many of these motives are learned and developed in social settings from childhood onwards.[86] The examples of leaders such as Gandhi and Mandela illustrate how leaders can contribute significantly to creating an atmosphere of trust that supports the feeling of sharing a common goal, common vision, and above all a unique spirit that causes people to do their utmost for a more general cause. The creation of such a spirit and its internalization through learning processes (mainly informal) is, in fact, the "bottom line" of leaders' influence, and can be clearly identified when analyzing many organizational and social systems, including business organizations. Walt Disney, for example, created a very specific spirit in the entertainment industry. He managed to inculcate in every worker, from the most menial of street cleaners through the boatmen to the operators of various installations, that they were actors in a play. In general, the terminology used belongs to the theater, the audience are "guests," and thus, in an organization that is a business in every sense, he created a spirit of the theater in which every member, in addition to his technical role, does his best to entertain and amuse, especially the children.[87] In sum, leaders such as those described here, each in the specific circumstances relevant to their times, created new **learned** norms. Hence, transformational leaders are simply a very special category of great educators, and the greater their influence the more their heritage becomes part of the learning process – at times, as in the case of some of the leaders mentioned here, generations after their death.

Where do transformational leaders draw their inspiration? How are they imbued with the creative strengths needed to generate transformational processes? Where and how do they acquire the ability to nurture relations that encourage development and promote more principled, more social, more moral ways of thinking and acting? All these are related to the personality elements that develop in the leader himself. Therefore, we will now examine the sources and processes underlying the growth of the abilities and motivations to be a transformational leader.

Chapter 5

⚜

The Development of Transformational Leaders

The child is father of the man

William Wordsworth

"I'll tell you," said Franklin Roosevelt to a friend during one of the difficult periods of his presidency (which was among the most dramatic in the history of the United States), "at night, when I lay my head on my pillow, and it is often pretty late, and I think of the things that have come before me during the day, and the decisions I have made, I say to myself – well I have done the best I could, and turn over and go to sleep."[1]

With this simple story Roosevelt illustrates what is perhaps the main key to his personality and his presidency – his complete confidence in himself. This fact was evident in his lifestyle, his behavior, and in the testimony of the people who worked with him. For example, he had the ability to cut himself off and rest. To the amazement of his aides, he could sleep for twelve hours in periods of great stress. In contrast to most presidents, who became visibly weaker and less robust from one year to the next during their presidency, Roosevelt looked happy and blooming until the last year, when he began to suffer with his heart. Anne O'Hare McCormick, a New York Times journalist, wrote specifically about this: "From one year to the next the president looks more at ease in all circumstances, more at home in his position than any leader of his time. His nerves are stronger, his temper cooler and more even. If he worries, he gives no sign of it."[2] This self confidence was radiated to the surroundings in a way that is almost indescribable. "We have a leader," announced the newspaper headlines a short time after he was elected. "Roosevelt stiffened the people's spines to face hardship," remarked historian Gary Wills, "and even if the hardship did not go away, people drew strength from the very cock of his head, the angle of his cigarette holder, the trademark grin that was a semaphore of hope."[3]

What was the source of Roosevelt's self confidence? From where did he draw his optimism and his unswerving faith in a better future? What was that inner strength of assurance that in the end the goal would be achieved, victory would come? All the evidence that appears in psycho-historical analyses and biographies, as well as the testimony of Roosevelt himself, lead to his childhood in Hyde Park, New York.[4] (Even when he was president, he used to go back to his childhood home to replenish his batteries. He visited Hyde Park about 200 times during his presidency.) Strikingly similar evidence on childhood as a source of inner strength, as the psychological basis of the transformational leader was presented by Mahatma Gandhi,[5] Nelson Mandela,[6] Theodor Herzl,[7] and many others, who said that their confidence in their ability to be leaders was formed in their early childhood. I will return later to the specific dynamics in childhood that formed this confidence. However, self confidence, firm as it may be, is not enough to make a transformational leader. Many people have self confidence and are able to lead people or influence them, but do not necessarily want to be leaders. To be a leader one must have **motivation** to influence, to be in a position of influence – a position of leadership. Thus, as with every form of human achievement, the two necessary conditions for leadership are **ability** and **motivation**. If we look at music, for example, it seems quite clear that a person without an ear for music (ability) cannot become a great musician. The same applies to motivation. Who has heard of the musician Nirghazy? He was a musical prodigy who served as the subject of intensive research by the head of the psychological laboratory in Amsterdam. He began to compose music before he was four years old. He had perfect pitch and an excellent musical memory, but, like many child prodigies, he never fulfilled the hopes placed in him. He simply got tired of it.[8] To actualize talent, you need motivation. This is true also of sports, science, and leadership. To be a leader, a person must first want it very much and have certain capacities (which will be specified later). However, given that these conditions are present, there is also a **developmental** element. Again, just as an ambitious musician who is trained by the best teachers and schools will reach much higher achievements than one who is equally gifted and motivated but grows up in less favorable conditions, there are circumstances and conditions that lead to differential development of people even if they have similar motivation and abilities. The formula for "creating" a leader thus includes motivation to lead, capacities relevant for leadership, and a certain developmental process. This is the general conceptual framework upon which I will elaborate. First I will discuss the motivational element and then the other two components.

THE MOTIVATION TO LEAD

One of the strongest motivations existing in the human repertoire is the motivation to be admired. This appears in the biographies of writers, actors, and artists as well as leaders, some of whom were very destructive in human history.[9] An analysis of the common factors at the basis of this desire points to a phenomenon known in the literature as "narcissistic deprivation." According to scholars,[10] the mother (or other caregiver) who adores the baby and answers its narcissistic needs fosters what is called the "grandiose self," which psychologists claim is essential for normal development.[11] After this stage in normal development, the "grandiose self" diminishes and consciousness of the existence of others develops, leading to a more complex and realistic conception of the self in relation to the family and social environment. The specific motivation to be a leader, it is argued, has its roots in deprivation at the developmental stage of the "grandiose self." The individual forms a strong desire to compensate for the deprivation, to seek the missing admiration, briefly, to be grandiose— famous and adored. This desire can be fulfilled in many different ways,[12] for example, by becoming an actor or singer who is "addicted" to the applause of an admiring audience or of course by being a leader. Narcissistic deprivation can become a force propelled by a vast unsatisfied hunger for admiration. Such leaders are mainly occupied with self-aggrandizement, with exploitative behavior, and have ears only for admiration.[13] It appears, therefore, that the idea of compensation can explain the sources of motivation of certain types of leaders who may be called "negative" (even if they are charismatic). The mechanism of compensation appears in the thinking of Freud and Adler,[14] and not by chance. These were physicians, whose thinking, even on psychological processes, was rooted in biological observation. They discerned that biological organisms have the ability to create compensatory processes. When a person is blinded in one eye, his other eye strengthens functionally to compensate for it. In the same way, different organs or limbs in the body find ways to compensate for the loss of others by improved functioning. This principle was applied to psychological processes. For example, Adler spoke of an inferiority complex as generating a dynamic of compensation. Put somewhat simplistically, a student who is weak in studies may aspire to excel in sports. The student attempts to compensate for what is lacking. Thus, for certain people leadership may be a type of compensation for a painful psychological deprivation. As described, this is a mechanism that can be identified repeatedly in leaders who are outstandingly narcissistic.

However, negative narcissistic leaders are not the majority of leaders. How, then, can we explain the motivation of positive leaders, particularly of transformational leaders, whose contribution to society is beyond doubt? The attitudes and behavior of the latter are characterized by a pro-social and moral approach that is not compatible with narcissistic pathology. (In the DSM – the diagnostic and statistical manual of mental disorders – narcissistic pathology is characterized by symptoms such as a sense of grandeur and exaggerated self-importance, a preoccupation with fantasies of success, power or brilliance, expectation for constant admiration, lack of empathy, and so forth.[15]) Many explanations have been offered. Zaleznik, for example, a Harvard professor and psychoanalyst who has both studied leaders and worked with them as a consultant, argues on the basis of his observations that the motivation to be a leader is often related to the absence of a father in childhood.[16] This absence might be physical (orphanhood) or psychological (the father was not there for the child for reasons such as divorce or prolonged absences from home). According to Zaleznik, some of these children aspire to "correct" the experience. They fantasize about a "corrected father," and one of the ways to do this is by turning themselves into caring and protective father figures. Becoming a leader makes this possible. Burns,[17] in analyzing historical leaders, identified a similar pattern and added an Oedipal explanation. Not only does the child experience the absence of a father, but also he is very close to the mother. This combination, says Burns, has several implications that are relevant to the development of leadership. According to the classic Freudian argument, the most important emotional development takes place as a result of the Oedipal conflict. This is a huge drama whose resolution forms an emotional turning point. The small child longing for his mother, aspiring for complete ownership of her, is in fact unconsciously competing with his father over the same desire. This is pure competition that has all the ingredients and causes for great hatred. But because hatred of the father entails guilt feelings that are unbearable for the child, the only way to resolve this terrible conflict is to identify with the father instead of trying to destroy him. Instead of getting rid of his father, the child wants to be like him, and thus the son and the father are on the same side; both of them "own" the mother. The Oedipal drama thus accelerates the son's socialization process and explains the increased importance of the father's role in the early years.[18]

In the absence of a father with whom to identify, the figure required for resolution of the Oedipal conflict is missing, and this intensifies the child's desire to become himself a kind of father protecting the mother. He, as it were, matures, undertakes responsibility, takes care of things, becomes important and significant in his own sight, and his confidence and self esteem grow. This theme appears in many myths and folk tales portraying children's fantasies of protecting and guarding their mothers from harm.

Although psychoanalytical explanations are often criticized as speculative (because it is hard to observe unconscious processes and certainly to measure them directly), the statistical evidence supporting these arguments is hard to ignore. For example, while collecting material for biographies of 24 British prime ministers, from Spenser Percival in 1809 to Neville Chamberlain in 1937, British scholar Lucille Iremonger[19] was surprised to discover that fifteen of them (66%) had lost a father in childhood. In the light of these findings, Iremonger examined the census records for the year 1921 and found that only about 2% of the general population had been orphaned in childhood. Research conducted by Elder[20] reveals a similar direction. The research was conducted among people whose childhood had been spent in the United States during the Great Depression. Children whose fathers were unemployed at that time were exposed earlier to responsibility and the need to cope with difficulties. They were found in significantly higher numbers to be occupying positions that require responsibility, such as managerial and supervisory roles. Similar findings were obtained from a sample of forty-five British CEOs of large companies. Almost half of them had lost a father when they were less than sixteen years old and as a result had been expected to take responsibility and cope with it successfully.[21] These expectations were internalized and became part of their motivation to occupy influential and responsible roles. Indeed, there is much evidence of the power of expectations in creating motivation in various spheres,[22] and just as the expectations of parents and teachers affect the motivation to make efforts in other fields of activity, the same is true of leadership.[23] It seems that many of these examples can easily be explained without the help of psychoanalytic theory. Simply, messages are transmitted, overtly or covertly, to certain children, conveying expectations that they will take responsibility, use initiative, and do all the things that characterize positive leaders. And these expectations are internalized and become inherent motivation to be in leadership roles. It is not necessarily related only to the figure of the father. Family dynamics in general affect the readiness for social or political involvement (and hence the likelihood of being in leadership roles). A study conducted in Cambridge, Massachusetts, found that children who came from families where there

was a great extent of strict supervision chose to keep away from active political or social involvement.[24] The family socialization thus increases (or
decreases) the willingness to be involved and to be a potential leader. The
biographies of leaders like Franklin Delano Roosevelt and Nelson Mandela
demonstrate the power of expectations in general and family expectations
in particular. Roosevelt grew up in an aristocratic home where there was
a long tradition, almost an imperative, to study at Groton and Harvard –
institutions that transmitted to their students that they were seen as the elite
who were expected to fill leadership roles. There was also a family tradition
of leadership. As an only son, he was the target of clear expectations. Not
surprisingly, in his early days at Harvard he was already the editor of the
university newspaper, and he began to be involved in public activity at the
age of twenty. Figures published for Eton (the British equivalent of Groton)
show that this is no coincidence. Over 75 (25%) of the 284 members who
served in the British cabinet between 1868 and 1995 were graduates of
Eton.[25] It may, of course, be argued that the fact of going to Eton is the
result of a kind of selection that begins at home. Such children absorb the
expectation that they will become leaders, and these expectations are internalized and become a motivational force. Nelson Mandela is an example of
development indicating similar psychological processes in totally different
life circumstances. Although he grew up in a rural area and had brothers
and sisters, practically speaking he was the only boy among his sisters
(he was the son of his father's third wife, and his two older brothers had
left the village years earlier). His father, who was a kind of tribal leader,
died when Nelson was only nine, and the evidence suggests that he was
expected, first by his father and later by others, to "take responsibility"
and be an active leader in the extended family and the community. The
mother of the teacher Jaime Escalante, the transformational leader, left
his father when Jaime was nine and went to live in another city. Jaime
grew up before his mother left his drunken, cheating father, hoping that
the clever and beloved child who in fact had no real father would take
upon himself "the father's responsibility."[26] Thus, positive leadership (of
which transformational leadership is the most salient expression), unlike
negative leadership (narcissistic) is not necessarily grounded in processes
of narcissistic compensation, but in long-term processes of internalizing
expectations and "building" a profile that prepares them for leadership
(this building process will be discussed later). A comparative analysis of
outstanding negative and positive charismatic leaders in history provides
evidence in support of this argument. Negative charismatic leaders, like
Hitler or Jim Jones, went through a childhood marked by the experience of
marginality; they did not see themselves as leaders during their childhood.

In some cases their leadership was revealed by chance and sometimes suddenly in one dramatic episode. For some of them, this revelation of their ability to influence people, their charisma, and the admiring response, literally saved their lives. Without this revelation they were, by their own testimony, on a downward slope toward suicide.[27] Leadership was a response to the deep deprivations in their personality. Therefore, they were virtually addicted to it and, in some cases, the addiction was obsessive. The fact that Manson projected his psychological desolation and misery onto his followers prevented him from suicide and saved him from obsessive thoughts of escape and death. He described it in the following way: "I often had the urge to get my things together and head for unknown places, but I was so caught up with those kids (the Manson "family") and the role I played in their lives, to leave them would have been like ripping my heart out."[28] The birth of Hitler as a leader took place in World War I. Before the war he lived in Vienna, trying his luck as an artist, but was not accepted for the academy, which hurt him deeply. He secluded himself from the company of others and lived a miserable life in cheap hostels in Vienna. Apparently he indulged in sexual perversions. He lived in constant fear of making a fool of himself, looking ridiculous, inferior, weak or inept, or failing or being humiliated. Leadership for him was confirmation – which he had never had before – that he was a man of worth. He demanded loyalty, admiration, and submission from those around him. As with Jim Jones and Charles Manson, the theme of death was pervasive. The closeness and attraction to death are not coincidental. Hitler was motivated by the feeling that death was stalking him. His birth as a leader emanated from his closeness to death. The evidence on his feelings indicates that he was really born again during his military service in World War I, when he excelled as a squad commander. War to him was a life-saving drug. He described it in the following way: "War is life, war is the origin of all things, any struggle is war."[29]

For transformational leaders, unlike those characterized by narcissistic deprivation, leadership is not a solution to psycho-pathological distress or exclusive confirmation of their value, as in extreme pathological cases. An examination of the life stories of transformational leaders, certainly the most outstanding ones, indicates that they developed in a long process of building layer upon layer. Their entrance into leadership roles as adults was in many cases described as a natural continuation of processes that had begun early in their lives. In addition to a sense of self worth and belief in one's own ability, there are other psychological qualities that are essential for a person to become a transformational leader in terms of both motivation and ability to lead.

ABILITY TO LEAD

The fact that certain people from childhood develop powerful motivation to be leaders (for the reasons described earlier) is clearly not enough in itself, just as it is not enough to aspire to be a pilot without good coordination or a great musician without a good ear for music. To bring the motivation to fruition, the individual has to possess the relevant capacities, which may then be developed to the required levels.

In the case of transformational leadership, the relevant basic capacity is contained in the concept "self confidence."[30] Harry Truman used to say: "I wonder how far Moses would have got if he had taken a poll in Egypt."[31] Truman faced unpopular and hard decisions that only a person with considerable self confidence could take. The Marshall Plan, the huge aid program to Germany after World War II, was not exactly popular among millions of Americans who wondered why they should help to rehabilitate the cruel enemy. However, Truman did not think in terms of popularity; he was sure that this was the right thing to do. The evidence that perhaps best illustrates his self confidence, his ability to judge matters independently, is his recognition of the State of Israel in 1948. Many in his government opposed this, fearing an Arab oil embargo, and especially the effect of such an embargo on the Marshall Plan (the Europeans were very dependent on Arab oil). Among those opposed was George Marshall himself, who was Secretary of State in the Truman government and whom Truman esteemed most highly. Despite this fact, and despite his deep emotional ties with Marshall, Truman decided against the opinion of his cabinet members.[32]

I mentioned earlier Nelson Mandela's self confidence and independence in establishing and stubbornly adhering to the Truth and Reconciliation Commission against the majority opinion, including the opinion of some of his closest friends, who wanted to revenge themselves on the whites.[33] Theodor Herzl needed great self confidence not only in order to insist on his attitudes and his path, which many opposed, but also to display conviction and certainty among world leaders, some of whom were declared anti-Semitic.[34] Ben Gurion will always be remembered in the history of Israel, due to the self confidence that enabled him to declare the establishment of the state at a specific historic moment that was perceived by most of those who opposed it as impossible. In fact, it was only great self confidence that enabled him to make such a dramatic decision in conditions of extreme loneliness.[35] Such self confidence and its projection to others are required not only for making hard decisions, but for giving people the feeling that there is a leader. Considerable historical and research evidence indicates clearly that the leader's self confidence is perceived by the followers as the most important characteristic of his leadership.[36]

What are the sources of this self confidence? Obviously there are genetic factors, inherent temperament variables that are part of the leaders' "programming." These aspects have been investigated increasingly in recent years.[37] At present, we do not possess a great deal of knowledge about them. However, there are characteristics formed in infancy, which is the period regarded by major psychological theorists as the formative one in human emotional development.[38] Some of these variables, because they are formed at such an early age, at the beginning of the individual's life, become basic developmental variables (like the genetic variables) and form the ground for the development of characteristics of leadership in the family, in the children's group, in the school, and later on in various personal experiences. Hence, apart from the genetic variables, development as a leader is built on two types of characteristics:

1. Characteristics formed in infancy, which become **basic components** of the developing ability.
2. Characteristics that develop in the course of life (contingent on the existence of the basic components).

I will first discuss the basic components and then the long-term developmental characteristics.

BASIC COMPONENTS IN THE ABILITY TO LEAD

A person who was the unchallenged love of his mother, claimed Sigmund Freud, has "the feeling of a conqueror, that confidence of success that often induces real success."[39] Indeed, the biographies of many outstanding leaders describe close and loving ties with the mother. Herzl's relationship with his parents was well known; they were behind him through all the ups and downs of his extraordinary life. Although they were assimilated Jews who were enamored of the European culture, especially the German culture, they supported him financially and morally in all his struggles for a Jewish state. In fact, they spent most of their assets on it. His mother, Jeanette, loved him boundlessly. In this respect, there was a great deal in common between Herzl and Freud. Both grew up during the same period and in the same Austro-Hungarian urban, Jewish bourgeois environment. Freud's mother said that "her baby was born in his placenta and therefore it was guaranteed that he would be famous."[40] She believed wholeheartedly in this forecast. Herzl's birth was accompanied by no such signs, but his mother was convinced from an early age that a great future awaited her son. His wealthy parents spared no effort to give him the best in education and culture. According to his own testimony (he wrote a lot in his diary), the love of his parents, especially his mother, was a huge support in his loneliness, the loneliness that is the fate of most great leaders.[41]

Mahatma Gandhi (who also wrote about his life) describes the deep love between himself and his mother. She was much younger than his father, who was always occupied with his public activities. Gandhi's mother was a religious woman, who fasted often, and lived an ascetic lifestyle, abstaining from luxury. Later Gandhi was to describe her as an angel, saying that the image of his mother was engraved in him; she was his compass in relating to people and to the world.[42] Although they lived in such culturally, and certainly financially, different environments, the family dynamics described regarding the lives of Franklin Roosevelt and Mahatma Gandhi are strikingly similar – two children of young mothers and older, successful fathers. They were two children who enjoyed much love from their mothers. Roosevelt, the aristocratic only son, was at home until the age of fourteen. His mother devoted herself to his education and care. Even as an adult when he went to live in Manhattan, his mother lived nearby and was beside him through most of the years while he was climbing the ladder of national leadership.[43] Nelson Mandela, too, describes experiences of great maternal love. In fact, he lived almost like the son of his father's four wives. They lived in the same locality, and they all got on well together. Mandela remarked to his biographer in describing his early childhood (up to the age of nine): "I had four loving mothers."[44] It is this relationship, this powerful emotional foundation created by the parents' love, especially the mother's love during infancy, that is the source of the confidence and the positive self esteem that find expression in the personalities of transformational leaders. The theoretical framework that describes this emotional development of self confidence most clearly is John Bowlby's attachment theory.[45]

The assumptions of attachment theory are based on evolutionary biological processes related to survival.[46] Most living creatures are equipped with the ability to fly, run, crawl, secrete venom, and so forth. Quite surprisingly, the human baby is completely helpless during infancy. His entire ability to survive depends on external help. To be fed, to be clean and not become ill with infectious diseases, to feel the world around him, the baby must have the help of adults, usually one of his parents, most often the mother. When the baby is hungry, thirsty, cold, hot, afraid, alarmed, all these primary feelings receive a response through the caregiver. This proximity to the caregiver is thus existential in the most basic senses; it is the primary instinctive basis for attachment.

Another possible explanation for attachment (the strong emotional relationship that the baby develops towards its parents – especially the mother) is connected to a phenomenon that was discovered by the Austrian scholar Konrad Lorenz.[47] In his observations of ducks, Lorenz discovered a phenomenon defined as "imprinting." When a newly hatched duckling discerns something moving, it follows it. If the duckling continues to follow that object for ten minutes, it becomes attached to it. In nature, the moving object is usually the mother duck. But Lorenz managed to prove in his research that ducklings might become attached by imprinting to a wooden duck on wheels, to a cardboard rectangle, and even to his rubber boots (when he walked in them). The ducklings followed these objects and related to them as if they were the natural mother – sought their proximity and quacked loudly when they moved away. Lorenz found that imprinting takes place very easily in the time span that he defined as the "critical period" (between two days and fifty-one hours). After the critical period, it is hard to create imprinting. The imprinting period was also found among other species, such as lambs and pups.[48]

Another answer to the question concerning what motivates primary attachment was given by a pair of American scholars,[49] who reached their ideas by chance. They were engaged in the study of learning processes and they conducted experiments on rhesus monkeys, whose development is regarded as very rapid and to a large extent similar to human behavior. To equalize the conditions of their growth and early experiences, the researchers separated the infant monkeys from their mothers immediately after birth and raised them in different cages, in each of which there was a terry cloth blanket. To their surprise, the young monkeys became so attached to the blankets that when these were taken away to be laundered they became very depressed. This discovery led to an examination of the importance of warmth. For this purpose, the researchers built two artificial "mothers," made of wire mesh. One of them remained exposed and was therefore called the wire mother, and a bottle of milk was attached to it. The other was covered with sponge and terry cloth and was called the cloth mother. The cloth mother had no feeding mechanism attached. When the baby monkeys grew up with these two "mothers," it emerged that they preferred the physical presence of the cloth mother. The physical contact with her provided them with warmth and security. These studies by the Harlows showed that warmth (through physical contact) is a primary need, that is, a very powerful need on a par with physiological needs such as hunger and thirst.

The total existential dependence on the caregiver according to evolutionary theory, the imprinting during the critical period according to the explanations of Lorenz and others, and the need for warming physical contact, especially in early infancy – all of these are the ground on which attachment theory is based as formulated by John Bowlby. This theory says that relations formed during the critical period have deep psychological significance. The dynamic of the infant's dependence and the caregiver's warmth and response to needs creates internal working models that will affect the individual's attitude to himself and to others throughout his life. When the caregiver is receptive and responsive to signs of distress from the baby (expressed in crying, etc.) and supplies the child's needs readily and with sensitivity, the baby, at the level of basic primary sensations, can feel that he has a **secure base**. How do we know this? We know this simply by observing behaviors.[50] For example, babies who have a sense of security reveal more explorative behaviors. They will dare to move further away from the caregiver, they will try to examine things, to touch things. On the other hand, when the caregiver is inattentive, insensitive, inconsistent, or simply tends to ignore the baby's distress signals. insecure patterns of attachment are formed. The early studies in this area refer to two attachment patterns formed in situations when the caregiver does not provide security: an ambivalent pattern and an avoidant pattern. The former develops as a result of inconsistency in relations with the caregiver, who is sometimes warm and sensitive, and sometimes simply not there. The latter is formed when the caregiver is not sensitive to, and even ignores, the infant's distress. In this case, the child expresses behaviors of avoidance, withdrawal, and loneliness.[51]

What is the connection between models and studies of infancy and the discussion on leadership relations? I have expanded on attachment theory in order to clarify the thinking that shows a clear connection between the internal world formed on a primary basis in childhood, and feelings, behaviors, and relations expressed by adults. Hundreds of studies[52] have found that the internal working models formed as a result of the type of primary relations in childhood are expressed in adulthood, particularly on the level of **emotionally significant relationships**. For example, a comparison of the three attachment patterns found that those with a secure pattern were able to maintain a greater degree of intimacy in spousal relations.[53] Similar findings were obtained with regard to the ability to maintain close and intimate relations with friends.[54] The common factor of all these findings is clearly the development of abilities, feelings, or internal models that are conducive to a positive view of the self and of others, to putting one's trust in others and giving to others in a way that does not only serve narcissistic needs.[55] Many important psychological theories have put forward similar arguments. For example, Eric Berne, a prominent psychoanalyst, describes "Games People Play."[56] The major concepts relating to these games are "scenarios" formed in early childhood. For example, in the scenario "I'm OK, You're OK," the child who received positive messages about himself and the world around him goes out into the world equipped with confidence and the ability to trust others. In contrast, there are negative scenarios in which the parents' behavior toward the child conveyed that he was "Not OK" or that others were "Not OK." In this case, the child goes out into the world bearing a large degree of suspicion and with limited ability to trust others. We see here that Berne's theory is close to the idea of the internal working model in attachment theory.[57] The fundamental argument is very clear: as leadership is a category of emotional relations, and emotional relations can be explained and predicted on the basis of internal models formed in early childhood, leader-follower relations can also be predicted in this way. This is borne out by studies conducted recently. Leaders who were found to be transformational received higher scores in the "secure pattern" measures. That is to say, their large measure of emotional security gave them the degree of confidence and openness required to maintain relations with others based on trust.[58] The secure style, or more precisely the psychological conditions that lead to the development of the secure style, also affect the level of optimism existing in the individual. Optimism, as we saw, is both a basic component in the ability to believe in the good in human nature and a necessary condition for the formulation of an exciting and optimistic vision (as we saw in the previous chapter). Although research on the sources of optimism is still in its early stages, from what we know so far optimism has both genetic roots and psychological roots formed in early childhood. For example, Plomin and colleagues[59] found in a study on 500 pairs of twins, half of whom were raised together and half separately, that the genetic component constituted 25% of the explanation for optimistic tendencies. As yet, there have been no long-term studies on this subject, but it was found that optimistic people remember their childhood as pleasant, recall that they were given considerable autonomy in childhood, and were encouraged to aspire and hope for good. They remember their parents as socially active, warm, and giving.[60]

When Gandhi was eleven years old, a British school inspector came to his school to test the level of teaching. For this purpose, he asked the students to spell five words that he dictated to them in English. No one made a mistake except Gandhi. The regular class teacher, who was walking around and looking at what the students had written, noticed the mistakes and urged Gandhi to copy from his neighbor. Gandhi did not do this. Later, the teacher spoke scathingly of his stupidity and of the fact that he had lowered the results of the class, but Gandhi thought that he had done the right thing.[61] This little story casts light on some important aspects of Gandhi's personality, which would be revealed when he eventually became a transformational leader. First, the self confidence needed in order not to go with the stream. In this case, it stands out particularly, because apart from the natural tendency to succeed, there was also legitimacy and even encouragement by the authority to act in such a way. Nevertheless, considering that it was not right, Gandhi remained true to himself, even at the cost of failure and mockery. Second, and this is the point that distinguishes outstanding transformational leaders, is their principled attitude toward people. Gandhi, in a retrospective analysis, remarked that the incident did not affect the respect that he continued to feel for that teacher. "I was," he said, "by nature blind to people's mistakes."[62] And his adult life showed that Gandhi was very accepting of others and imbued with belief in the good in human nature. When he began to work as a young lawyer in South Africa, he represented a rich man (Dada Abdallah, who had brought him to South Africa) who was suing a debtor who owed him a huge sum. It was a clear case in legal terms and would have completely ruined the debtor's business. Despite the assured legal success, Gandhi persuaded his client to settle the debt in payments in order not to ruin his rival. Only in this way could Gandhi find his mission as an attorney, and thus he wrote in his diary: "I learned the true mission of the law, I learned to see the good sides of human nature and penetrate into the hearts of people." And in evaluating the success of this case, which was transformative in terms of his self concept as a lawyer, he said: "Not only did I not lose anything, I remained true to my soul."[63] This was also a salient characteristic in the personality of Nelson Mandela, whose forgivingness and acceptance of others (including his enemies) was part of his worldview, as he said: "Brave people are not afraid to forgive in order to achieve peace."[64] In a psychological analysis it is easy to discern that this quality was imprinted and developed in Mandela from early childhood. Even as a young child, and increasingly as he grew older, Mandela showed a large measure of self confidence, a large measure of basic optimism, and a large measure of trust in human nature. One of his aides, Ahmed Kathrada, claimed that many of those who came to his doorstep when he was nominated president were manipulative, treacherous schemers. But Mandela refused to be suspicious, he insisted on rising above this and focusing on positive messages.[65]

It seems, therefore, that the psychological characteristics of self confidence and optimism are necessary, but in order to be relevant for leadership (whose most basic meaning is involvement in social contexts) they have to be accompanied by care for others and the inclination to act for the good of society. Indeed, it was found that the ability to be empathetic is the basis for social and moral behavior. Without compassion, without the ability to feel and identify with the suffering of others, there cannot be pro-social behavior.[66] This ability is essential for a person to be a leader in the social context in general and certainly a transformational leader. Developmental psychologists who attempted to examine the sources of empathy, the components and processes at the basis of pro-social behavior, found that this characteristic, too, is composed of both genetic components and components that develop in early childhood.[67] In general, it was found that parents who were warm, sensitive, and attentive to the needs of their small children, who were themselves models of pro-social behavior, raised children who as adults were more empathetic and more oriented to the distress of others.[68] Thus, we see that the emotional and behavioral factors that form the secure attachment style are also the factors that lead to the development of the other basic components of transformational leadership: care and concern for others, and optimism, which is the starting point for leading people forward to a better future.

Obviously, many people who are not leaders have these characteristics, but the evidence regarding transformational leaders indicates that from these basic components, the ability to be a transformational leader continues developing.[69] Leadership does not develop in infancy, but that is when the psychological foundations are laid for further development. We will now turn to examine how leadership continues developing in later stages of life.

DEVELOPMENTAL PROCESSES OF LEADERSHIP

As stated, the assumption is that individuals with similar ability and motivation can develop differently and at different paces because of different conditions as well as events that take place in the course of their lives, in the family, at school, in the company of other children, and in the social and political environment in general.[70] The fact that Roosevelt was sent to Groton and Harvard obviously had an enhancing effect on the motivation and ability to lead that were imprinted in him. Hence the discussion is on the aspects that enhance the development of leadership, that cause the ability and motivation to ripen. Moreover, my argument is that the basic components (genetic components and psychological components developed in infancy), which differ in their intensity, will be important in determining the speed and intensity of the processes that can develop leadership.

The primary learning of leadership appears to take place, according to the evidence of leaders themselves, through observation of or exposure to models of leadership.[71] For example, Mahatma Gandhi's father was prime minister of a province in India. The young Mahatma was able to observe daily a model of involvement and leadership, and because he admired and respected his father, this observation became powerful social learning.[72] Nelson Mandela had a similar experience, growing up in a village and observing his father who was a local leader.[73] The fact that in both these cases the father died when they were young boys may perhaps have intensified their influence. At all events, according to their own testimony, the existence of a "leadership model" in the family carried weight in their future development. In the family of Franklin Roosevelt there was also a leadership model who was a source of admiration and pride for the entire family – Theodore Roosevelt, the distant uncle who was an outstanding and vibrant president at the beginning of the twentieth century. Jaime Escalante, who became an educational leader, had a model in the person of his maternal grandfather, who was a retired teacher and philosopher and used to play and talk with him a lot during his childhood in the village. This theme of a leadership model in the family environment appears in the biographies of many leaders, and served as a model for imitation in varying degrees.[74]

The exposure to role models and processes, especially during childhood, also has influence on the development of beliefs and outlooks that are less amenable to observation and empirical measurement but reach clear expression in leadership, because they are the basis for the visions and messages transmitted by transformational leaders, as well as for everyday behavior. Mandela grew up in an atmosphere of "ubuntu" (an African term similar to "human brotherhood"). Often he would quote a famous African wise man who said "A man is a man because of other people." Or, relating to leadership, he always said: "You cannot do anything if you do not have the support of other people."[75] These beliefs, which were the foundation of Mandela's style of working, grew out of his observation of the rural community where he grew up. In telling his biographer of the sources of the development of his worldview, he said: "People like ourselves brought up in a rural atmosphere get used to interacting with people at an early age."[76] Mandela himself connected this to his worldview, which later found political expression: "People are human beings, produced by the society in which they live. You encourage people by seeing the good in them."[77] Mandela had observed political institutions that operated in this spirit and without doubt, this influenced him when he became a leader. For example, he saw how the village council operated. In his memories of himself as a curious child the important political procedure in the village was as follows: "The village council was completely democratic, that all the members of the tribe could participate in its deliberations. Chief and subject, warrior and medicine man, all took part and endeavored to influence its decisions. It was so weighty and influential a body that no step of any importance could ever be taken by the tribe without reference to it."[78] And when he was a revered leader many years later, he tended (too much, according to his detractors) to act always by consensus.

We can see how Gandhi's worldview was built and developed out of the basic components that were engraved in him in early childhood, and how this outlook became an element in the political struggle to free India through non-violent civil resistance. The major aspects of this outlook were belief in the power of truth (satigyara), and the power of spirituality (brahamcharia). In explaining the supreme importance of spirituality, he said: "Life without brahamcharia is low and bestial. The animal by nature cannot conquer its desires and a human is called a human only because he is able and in fact does conquer his desires."[79] When we look for the sources of this development we can find it in his mother. Once, when he was asked by his secretary about the influences in his life, he distinguished between austerity and saintliness in relating to his mother, he saw in her a model of saintliness, of spirituality. His mother who was imprinted in him turned spirituality into a way of life that was both personal and political.

The basic components described here not only influence the way in which learning and imitation models are perceived; they affect the actual selection of the exposure to every stimulus that affects the leaders' worldview. In other words, people with different basic components will be exposed to different stimuli. For example, one of the books that most influenced Gandhi's worldview as a political leader was John Ruskin's *Unto this Last*. He read it on a train on one of his journeys in South Africa. According to his testimony, he could not close his eyes after reading this book: "I was ready to change my life according to the ideas presented in the book," he said.[80] The main argument of the book is that the true basis of society is not wealth, as the classic economists think, but companionship. Gandhi was also strongly influenced by Tolstoy. Scion of a wealthy landowning family, Tolstoy turned his back on wealth at the age of fifty-seven and went to live with beggars. He refused the Nobel Prize (because he refused to accept money). The two corresponded, writing long letters to each other. Tolstoy's outlook on simplicity appealed to Gandhi.[81] It seems that we can see quite clearly how the outlooks of Mandela and Gandhi began to develop in early childhood (which created selective prominence or attractiveness for other specific developmental components later). However, an examination of the history of many leaders shows that these are not special cases in terms of development, but examples of typical developmental patterns. In other words, the basic components are both the catalyst and the filter for frames of reference and models from which people learn about leadership.

But it is not only exposure to models or interactions that is the source of development. From developmental psychology we know that one of the most important sources of learning is **experience**. In fact, many leaders state that experience is the best teacher. There is much research evidence for this. John Kotter,[82] who interviewed 200 managers, leaders of successful companies, noted that the important sources of leadership development, based on their retrospective reports, were: 1) being assigned challenging roles at the beginning of their management career; 2) task force assignment; 3) special tasks or projects that they were asked to perform beyond their ongoing work; 4) experience of various training simulations, namely, personal experiences from which they learned about themselves in the context of their leadership.

Other leaders, in analyzing those moments in their past when they felt that they had been able to influence others, referred to a variety of experiences. Some spoke of family situations in which they had taken care of their siblings, others spoke of situations when they had "discovered" in the youth movement, in school, or in neighborhood games, that people tended to listen to them more than to others, waited for them to "organize things," and so forth.[83] These experiences not only showed them that others saw them as leaders but strengthened their own belief in their ability to be leaders. This psychological variable, known as self efficacy, is of major importance in understanding the development process of leaders. Self efficacy is the individual's perception with regard to his abilities in certain spheres, and according to many studies conducted by Albert Bandura,[84] and other scholars following him, it is largely determined by the degree to which the person believes that he has succeeded in previous performances in that sphere. Successes in performance thus create high expectations for success in future performances, high self efficacy, and when these expectations are internalized, even chance failures do not change the belief in one's ability. On the other hand, a person who has experienced many failures or painful ones in a certain sphere will have lowered self efficacy, to the extent that he may avoid action in that sphere.[85] A biographical analysis of many leaders clearly indicates the development of self efficacy in management. Gandhi was a shy and introverted child (though not lacking in self confidence). His belief in his ability to be a leader was constructed in the course of his stay in South Africa when he worked as a lawyer and gradually became leader of the Indian community there. His self efficacy was constructed on the basis of his approach as a lawyer, an approach whose main principle was not to trample on the other side. For example, in one of his early cases in South Africa he represented an Indian laborer who had been beaten by his employer and had two of his teeth broken. Gandhi sued the employer, but also settled with him that the worker would switch to a new employer. He acquired a reputation as someone who was not vengeful but sought the benefit of all sides without distorting the truth. This professional reputation, alongside his image as an honest and spiritual person, made him a figure whom the Indians in South Africa began to see as a moral authority. And thus, gradually, at first in sporadic public events and later as secretary of the Indian community in South Africa, he began to be built up as a leader. When he returned to India after twenty-one years in South Africa, his path as national leader was open, but beyond that, his self efficacy as a leader was firmly set.[86]

Other studies on leaders of organizations, based on biographical analyses or the leaders' memories of their development process, indicate a similar pattern. Their self efficacy as leaders[87] was built up out of past experiences, most of them at an early age.[87] However, self learning based on personal experience contains another assumption that cannot be separated from the basic components described above – the leaders' ability to reflect on themselves and their surroundings without a distorted wrapping of defenses, to see themselves from the outside as others see them, in broad daylight. This is an ability not possessed by narcissistic leaders, for example, who are motivated by self-aggrandizement. The testimonies of such leaders reveal that they surrounded themselves with blind admirers and demanded constant flattery.[88] The element of self confidence in its basic psychological senses has significant weight in learning ability and self development, particularly as regards self criticism. Bennis,[89] who studied the sources of development of outstanding leaders in various organizations, found that these leaders had exceptional ability to reflect on themselves as well as interested observation of the world around them. This is consistent with the findings of developmental psychology on the effect of the secure attachment style.[90] One of the major arguments of attachment theory is that people with a secure attachment style are characterized by more explorative behaviors. They are less afraid to try new things; they venture more to satisfy their curiosity. The research literature on transformational leadership also reports findings that transformational leaders become catalysts of intellectual stimulation; they are not only curious, they are not afraid to test their assumptions and attitudes and lay them open to critical discussion. Thus we see here conceptual and empirical proximity whose practical meaning is one: people with more self confidence (whether defined in clinical terms such as low level of anxiety, or in concepts of psychology of the self) are people who are more open to experience, who seek learning experiences, but more important, they learn more about themselves from these experiences because they are less defensive. Moreover, their psychological security allows them to be more open to environmental stimuli. In Bennis' study on the development of organizational leaders – people who are perceived as pragmatic, as performance oriented doers par excellence – it emerged from their self reports on their development that they had learned a great deal about leadership by studying human nature. It was the more anthropological observations of the nature of cultures, the attempt to trace patterns of thinking and behavior, to discover the sources of people's enthusiasm, which they reported as having special value in the leaders' development. Another aspect in the development of leaders is the behavioral one, and this has been examined extensively, particularly in the American research literature, which is very empirical and focused on behaviors. The guiding principle of behavior theory is the law of effect, which says that behavior is guided by past results. If a certain behavior was rewarded in the past (positive reinforcement), it will be repeated, according to the theory. And if the behavior met with punishment (negative reinforcement), it will almost certainly not be repeated. Thus, behaviors that are random to begin with, on a trial and error basis become deliberate if rewarded or disappear if not.[91] Thus, in addition to the strengthening of self efficacy through success in concrete experiences, people will tend to adopt behaviors that bring them positive reinforcement (appreciation, respect, etc.). This basic learning principle (on which thousands of studies on behavioral learning have been conducted) is perhaps especially relevant to the sphere of leadership in being extended to vicarious learning – a major principle in Bandura's social learning theory.[92]

Social learning theory is an extension of behavioral learning theories that argue that learning is generated by reinforcement. Social learning theory extends this argument to include indirect reinforcement. For example, there will be a greater tendency to imitate characters in films and plays, or people observed in social contexts such as the school or youth movement, or even characters in books, when these figures receive positive reinforcement of various kinds. In other words, observation of behaviors that are rewarded makes these behaviors worthy and even worthwhile imitating, because the chances of reward are seen as much greater.[93] In the context of learning "leadership behaviors," children who are exposed to leadership models who receive positive reinforcements – appreciation, respect, esteem – will tend to imitate these behaviors. Hence, exposure to models of leadership who receive positive reinforcements can have a developmental effect, certainly on the level of behaviors.

In conclusion: it appears that the development of leaders is a complex combination of genetic elements and acquired characteristics. Somewhat arbitrarily, I divided the variables into "basic components," which include both the genetic elements and those that develop in infancy, and emotional variables that create the infrastructure for further development (e.g., the secure style). On the basis of these variables, developmental processes occur, such as experience of responsible roles (e.g., as a result of a certain family situation), or success in leadership experiences in various social frameworks. These reinforce the belief in one's ability (self efficacy) to lead. In addition, exposure to models of leadership in the family and social environment, as well as vicarious learning, reinforce leadership behaviors. Furthermore, a worldview that is a basis for leadership messages develops in interactions with various stimuli in the social environment. The salience and attractiveness of these stimuli are largely determined by the aforementioned basic components. There is no evidence that motivation to lead is genetic. Apparently, the reverse is true, this motivation is formed and develops in life circumstances, regarding whose patterns there is initial evidence.[94] There are today some studies examining the genetic elements of leadership.[95] However, we still lack concepts and research tools for examining the relative weight of the genetic and acquired factors. Insofar as one can judge, as with other spheres such as music, sports, or science, it is a question of interaction between the two (the genetic and the acquired), and, therefore, it is necessary to relate to both. However, as I have tried to show, this should not be viewed dichotomously, but as two components, which combine to form a whole that is greater than the parts, like a musical composition that is greater than the individual notes of which it is composed.

Chapter 6

Conclusion

One of the interesting questions about ideas and how they stand the test of time concerns the rise and fall of ideas dealing with man and society, and the centrality of these ideas. Why do certain theories become central, and later (some of them quite quickly) lose their charm. I mentioned this briefly in the introductory chapter, in referring to the circumstantial context of the discussion on leadership theories. Here, in this concluding chapter I wish to reopen the question in a broader context, in order to place the specific discussion on leadership in a wider perspective of observation, before going on to examine the inferences and meanings related to the leadership phenomenon itself, as discussed and analyzed in the book.

For hundreds of years the theoretical discussion on man has, in different ways, touched on the dynamics of man vis-à-vis nature. Beyond the different terminologies used by philosophers, theologians, and others, nature was depicted as hell, in the sense that millions of people died of epidemics, or were fatally hit by natural disasters. As the way of life was based mainly on farming, fishing, and hunting, the people's livelihood was largely dependent on "luck" with regard to the workings of nature. This approach has changed dramatically in the western world, especially in the twentieth century. The life expectancy has risen from thirty in the nineteenth century to over seventy today. The advances in science, medicine, and technology have not only more than doubled the life expectancy, they have also changed the way people live, the occupational structure, the world of values, but mainly, they have changed the approach to the question of existence: man has gained mastery over nature! Hell is no longer nature and its vagaries, as Jean Paul Sartre remarked sarcastically: Hell is other people.[1]

In this state of affairs, the focus of the theoretical discussion shifts to the social context. It is impossible to imagine the appeal of the ideas of Karl Marx or Sigmund Freud before man and the social environment (and not nature) came to be seen as the center of existence, and thus of attention and interest. The interest in theories on leadership is a part of this process. There are hundreds of definitions of leadership,[2] but beyond the divisions and debates over the "true definition," all those concerned with the study of leadership agree that the minimal necessary definition is that "a leader is someone who has followers." This simple statement is the basis for all the rest, and its meaning is that leadership is a social phenomenon with sociological and psychological significance. Hence, in an era when there is growing interest in theories dealing with social phenomena, a phenomenon such as leadership takes a more central place in the discussion. The daily rhetoric in the press, on television and radio, as well as the large quantities of academic writing and research, indicate the intensified occupation with leadership.[3] Moreover, observation of the contents of the discourse on leadership indicates that leadership among humans is unique in that it can be discussed and researched only in terms characteristic of humans. There are, in fact, writers who analyze leadership in comparison with or in relation to other animals.[4] It is true that one can see "leadership" among animals, true that a herd of goats follows the leading goat, but these analogies cannot be stretched beyond their limits. The systematic study of leadership deals with factors such as charisma, leaders' rhetoric, symbolism, psychological processes, and emotions (including the unconscious). All these factors are not given to comparison, and certainly not to observation, in the case of leadership in nature. In this respect, we are dealing with the study of a phenomenon whose sources and order could not be examined at all if it were not a human and social phenomenon, that is to say, capable of verbal report.

What can we learn from all the analyses, examples, and research studies presented in this book? As usual, there are some more important and some more marginal inferences. The more marginal, in my opinion, concern the over-emphasis on the daily behavior of leaders, without a much broader perspective of period, circumstances, or intentions. For example, John Kennedy lied on many occasions,[5] but even his lies have different connotations if we look at the context. He lied about his health when he enlisted in the navy in order to serve in World War II (he had a glandular disease known as Addison's disease, which would have disqualified him for military service). Most people would call this a white lie, but Kennedy also lied about other things, about his affairs with women, and even about seemingly trivial things, like his reading speed, which was the talk of the town in Washington (it was estimated that he read 1,200 words a minute, which is twice the average). At a party, his sister, Eunice Shriver, told Times editor Henry Luce how quickly her brother read, after training at a speed reading institute. Galbraith, the famous economist, said in an interview that Kennedy had read a twenty-six-page memo from him in ten minutes, that is, about 1,000 words per minute (clearly we have no way of knowing whether he read the document carefully). When Kennedy realized that he had acquired this image, he took care to foster it. Investigation revealed that Kennedy had never visited the speed-reading institute.[6] This small, and perhaps silly story teaches us something more important than the tendency of certain leaders to magnify themselves, even by white lies. What seems to me the important lesson is the human desire, or perhaps need, to foster "leadership legends." The sources of this tendency are connected with all of the types of explanations presented in this book: the inherent longing for a big strong figure, the innate need for meaning, the need for symbols and social distinctions. In these contexts, the collective consciousness is aided by legends. Almost every transformational leader that we can point to, certainly those mentioned in this book as examples of transformational leadership, had behavioral flaws. They were not legends; they were people with strengths and weaknesses. Sometimes they were petty, sometimes they were unfaithful in their personal relationships, and sometimes they were disagreeable, moody, and so forth. Certainly leaders, even great ones, are subject to whims and human weaknesses, but their leadership should be seen and evaluated in a broader and more comprehensive context. James McGregor Burns, perhaps the most eminent writer on leadership, distinguishes between ethical and moral leadership.[7] Being an ethical leader means being a role model. A role model type of leader, in my opinion (and that of other scholars), is a critical necessity in close relationships, from marriage and parenthood to leadership in communities or organizations. The ethical leader maintains familiar standards and demonstrates their application in his daily behavior (I refer the reader to the discussion of role modeling in the chapter "Transformational Leadership," citing Bernard Bass's leadership questionnaire, in the context of the factor "idealized influence").

Moral leadership is leadership oriented to the highest values of society. It is evaluated less in terms of personal behavior. Such leaders bring about the formation of new laws, game rules, and modes of action that make society more just and more moral. The documents and laws inspired by Franklin Roosevelt, such as the Bill of Rights, the Economic Bill Of Rights, or the

Four Freedoms, and equally, the ability to integrate these principles at the level of everyday life, make Roosevelt and others like him transformational leaders. We see, then, that not all ethical leaders are transformational, and there are transformational leaders who have flaws in their ethical behavior.

The example of Franklin Roosevelt is an illustration of a bias, which I have barely touched upon in this book, the creation of leadership legends. One of the tendencies in this context is over-estimation, not only by followers but also by "experts" of leaders' intellectual abilities. For example, during the years of Roosevelt's political activities, fierce ideological debates raged around the idea of laissez faire, which was the dominant ideology. There were some prominent thinkers who attacked this thinking. One of them, Thorstein Veblen, argued that unadulterated capitalism is completely ineffective when it comes to building armies, schools, and so forth. Roosevelt had not read those books; he used to talk to people (he particularly enjoyed talking to Walter Lipmann, a sharp-eyed journalist who was also an idealist). His decisions were based on intuition and a sense for people.[8] David Ben Gurion, undoubtedly a transformational leader, used to say that he was "an expert on experts." This intuition is hard to define, but it is clearly related to the ability to identify patterns, to separate the wheat from the chaff, and includes a kind of compass showing the right proportions between the abstract and the practical, between fantasy and possibility.

Here is another point that is somewhat overlooked in the daily discussion on leaders – the motives of some of them may often be different from what people tend to attribute to leaders who make a positive contribution to society. When John Kennedy was murdered after being president for only three years, one of those closest to his shocked brother, Robert Kennedy, said that Julius Caesar was also assassinated after "only" three years in office. "But," replied Robert Kennedy, "Julius Caesar had Shakespeare."[9] True, some leaders are motivated to do great things by their desire to go down in history. Nevertheless, in a broader context, the leadership of some of the transformational leaders, and certainly the examples cited in this book, constituted a meaningful step towards what the German philosopher Hegel called the "spirit of wisdom," advancing the world towards wiser values.[10] Although Lincoln did not see himself at the beginning of his presidency as fighting to abolish slavery, his leadership advanced the subject of equality, or more precisely, contributed significantly to the growing delegitimization of discrimination. Although, even one hundred years after Lincoln's time a black leader was murdered in the struggle for equality, it is most likely that Martin Luther King's form of struggle, the arguments he used, and the support he won, could not have existed without Lincoln's contribution to

American history. Today it is hard to imagine the possibility of a university refusing openly and formally to admit an outstanding student simply because he is black, as happened in the mid-1960s in the southern states of the United States. This does not necessarily mean that people's stereotyped ideas have changed radically, but in democratic countries like the United States the discussion on questions of equality is no longer at the constitutional level. This in itself, from a historical viewpoint, is progress in the spirit of wisdom.

Some of the founding generation in the United States (and the writers of its constitution) were themselves slave owners who had not, in fact, experienced democracy. Although they had progressive ideas compared with the "old world" (Europe) from which they came, most of them were far from seeing the state as bearing social responsibility. On the contrary, if they had any doubt (and some did, obsessively), it was that the state might intervene too much in the lives of its citizens. Their attitude was one of "live and let live," let people make use of their abilities and live their lives. Furthermore, the American life style was influenced by ideas like those of Adam Smith, who formulated a theory on the functioning of the free market based on man's "real nature." From the earliest times, according to Adam Smith, man has been motivated by instrumental interests. The principle guiding human behavior is pure and simple self interest. Or, as Smith phrased it: "It is not thanks to the enlightenment of the butcher or baker that we can expect our supper but to their self interest."[11] True, this spirit, among other things, enabled families to accumulate vast wealth and reach levels of affluence that were unprecedented in human history.[12] It was precisely the wealthy Franklin Roosevelt, the symbol of the WASP par excellence, who wrought a dramatic change in the perception of the state's responsibility. "Dear Mr. Roosevelt," wrote Eva Connors to the president on January 4, 1935, "You, a person born to riches and high social status, have become close to us, the poor who are occupied with our everyday concerns. Mr. Roosevelt, allow me to call you by a slightly different title: the *People's President* of the United States."[13] Indeed, the steps that Roosevelt took, although they sprang from pragmatic considerations based on a specific history, became irreversible in terms of the social consciousness – a clear trend in the direction of more responsibility on the part of the state in the spheres of infrastructure, health, education, and public insurance. It seems, then, that observation of intentions or motives or daily behaviors without a broad perspective can yield at best a partial picture, and at worst, distortion of leadership. After all, it is easy to criticize egocentric characteristics, it is easy to impute egocentric intentions to leaders if we relate only to their personality. But it is much harder to criticize an egocentric intention that leads to achievements that clearly meet the criteria of transformational leadership – particularly in the area of empowerment and social and moral development. Taken to extremes, it may be said, as a certain writer on leadership expressed it,[14] "even distinct Machiavellians can advance Platonic ideas." In other words, even leaders who are motivated by personal ambition "to build themselves monuments" can promote noble ideas. This is evident on the political level, but it also exists at the level of organizations and various social systems. It is a complicated point, because it appears to give greater weight to the result than to the intention. The difficulty in adopting this rule for judgment and evaluation has been examined in psychology,[15] and is rooted in the fact that the result may be not merely coincidental but even totally unrelated to the process that preceded it. Furthermore, the intention does not always include the range of possible results; sometimes the results simply arise out of developments whose force nobody imagined. During his climb to the position of national leader, there were not many who thought that Hitler's intentions were too dangerous, or that the results of his leadership would be so disastrous. Most of the people, including those who had not voted for him, saw him as a leader whose intentions were not particularly malicious and certainly not so satanic. Presumably many more would have opposed him if they had envisaged the results of the destruction that he brought upon the Germans themselves. It appears, therefore, that short term results are not in themselves a sufficient test, but nor does the intention, as we have seen, constitute an accurate prediction, and is sometimes even misleading.

In discussions that I hold with various groups, many speak with nostalgia of David Ben Gurion, the great leader, in contrast to the "little leaders" of today, who do not succeed in changing the dismal reality. In general, many speak of the leadership crisis in the west. They yearn for leaders like Churchill, De Gaulle, Ben Gurion, Roosevelt – leaders who are perceived as giant figures, and if they existed today, "the world would look different," as many say. For myself, I wonder whether David Ben Gurion would even have been elected today. When I play with this hypothetical possibility I wonder who he would speak to today. For example, when I analyze the subjects that recur almost obsessively in all of his speeches, it would be hard to find a very broad public that is concerned today with the "ingathering of the exiles" and the "cultural melting-pot," with "making the desert bloom," and "redeeming the land" through physical labor. In a society that rejects the idea of the melting pot and prefers the image of the multicultural mosaic, in a country where the ultimate expression of the socialist pioneering ethos – the kibbutz – is in danger of extinction, in a place where the culture heroes are high-tech professionals, it is hard to see many potential voters whose emotions would be touched by Ben Gurion's speeches that were so inspiring in his day. He was a leader in a period when the major challenges were different, the society was in a different place in terms of historical development. Similarly, South African society today is not concerned with the struggle against apartheid, which was the focus of Mandela's leadership. And in the example often quoted, the British did not want to be led by a warrior like Churchill after the war. A gray lusterless leader without charisma like Clement Attlee was perceived as relevant for dealing with the task of rehabilitating the economy. Thus we return to the interactive and integrative nature of the leadership phenomenon. It is not possible to analyze leadership without relating to the circumstances, the followers and the leaders, and above all, the pattern of the interactions that arises out of this conjunction. The important analysis is, therefore, the analysis of this gestalt. Here, too, the principle is more evident in the case of prominent political figures, but the observation is relevant also to leadership in other, smaller frameworks. The literature contains many examples of leaders who were known as innovators, as groundbreakers, and yet failed later.[16] It is not that they lost their charisma; it is simply that the leadership challenges changed, the circumstances were different. The research literature dealing with organizational leaders is divided on the question of whether leaders should be "suited" to the situation or whether this is unimportant because leaders are supposed to change the situation. I believe that it is not a question of a dichotomy, but of a process in which the major leadership challenges are changing. These challenges derive from the situation (e.g., the type of task) and from the profile of the followers. A leader, certainly a transformational leader can (by definition) change many things, can change expectations, perceptions, the order of values, self efficacy, and so forth, but s/he cannot change all this without the understanding (which is not always purely cognitive) of the people and the circumstances in which s/he acts. The history of leaders in all areas of life reveals many examples of this argument.[17]

There is another added value in transformational leadership, which is rarely mentioned in the discussion on such leaders: the duration of their influence. Outstanding transformational leaders have long-lasting influence. In one book[18] there is a caricature showing Abraham Lincoln leading Theodore Roosevelt, who is leading Franklin Roosevelt. Here, we see that a picture is worth a thousand words. Lincoln's transformative influence lasted scores of years after his death, inspiring other presidents in a chain. The leaders themselves are not always conscious of this at the time, but it comes to light in a retrospective analysis of some of these leaders, and much can be learned from it. I emphasize this point because of the dominant tendency for short-term thinking and action in all areas. Parenthood is perhaps the simplest and most salient example to illustrate this point. As mentioned, there are few roles more transformational than that of parent. The more important theories in psychology (e.g., the theories of Sigmund Freud, Erik Erikson) are based on this simple idea. Yet, it is the short-term, mundane problems that are uppermost in the minds of most people, they are what dictate the routine, which itself has a transformational effect. In the case of leaders, too, there is a similar dynamic, perhaps even stronger, due to the nature of large systems. Political leaders want to be elected, and therefore they are eager to show their potential voters quick and even spectacular results. This pressure is even more intense in political systems in which the leader has a public of voters who "send" him to represent them. Then he is expected to show results in the period of a given term of office, otherwise his very election is in danger. The same dynamic prevails in big business concerns. Managers are tested by their results over a fairly short term. They have to show the board of directors and the stockholders a bottom line of profit – and quickly. As a result of the pressure they are apt to take measures such as reducing operating costs, firing workers, outsourcing, and similar steps, which improve the balance in the short term, but are often harmful (sometimes fatally so) in the long term, simply due to the loss of experience and talent, and above all of commitment and belief in the system.[19] In public organizations where leadership roles are based on terms of office (e.g., in the military), there is more often a tendency to employ one of two strategies: either "management by exception active" (see Bass's full range of leadership),[20] that is, trying to avoid mistakes in order to "get through the term in peace," avoiding taking any initiative, which might create hazards. This strategy at best preserves the status quo. The alternative strategy is to try to make a visible mark while in office – again an orientation for short-term action.

Nelson Mandela stretched out his arms to his rivals and even his jailers (he appointed the warden of the jail in which he had been incarcerated to a national post), despite the fact that in the short term his behavior and decisions in these matters were, to say the least, unpopular, angered many people, and could hurt him electorally. A review of the extensive literature on exceptionally successful organizations[21] reveals that what they all have in common are values imprinted by the leader of the organization. Many of the organizations described have operated with brilliant success for dozens of years, long after the death of the leaders. These, then, were leaders who influenced the *spirit* of doing things – aspects that are much more abstract and emotional than the bottom line in the balance of a given year. These influences have been compared to the design of a genetic code or basic assumptions (in the psychoanalytic sense).[22] Companies such as Disney or Ford are an illustration of these arguments.

As noted, the large number and type of factors involved in the discussion on leadership can be explained through the sociological prism of the changes in western society, the weakening and even disintegration of the formal authorities, the ascendance of personal freedom. This is a period unlike any that preceded it in human history. Most of the people in the west, especially in North America, live in conditions that would have seemed imaginary to people from other periods. The material wealth permits the acquisition and consumption of an amazing variety of products and services, the market mechanism permits almost unlimited choice in consumption. Furthermore, the autonomy, the freedom, and the possibilities go far beyond the material sphere. In the sphere of work there is unprecedented mobility both in careers and in the geographic space. People today are not limited by their work as were their parents, who in many cases worked in the same job and the same place throughout their lives. Almost everything is possible today even as regards personal life. Religious, geographical, and ethnic boundaries, and even sexual identities, can be crossed. Moreover, people can decide more than ever in the past whether they want children or not, whether they want them early or late in life, whether to give birth to them or adopt them, whether to raise them in an ordinary family in the "old tradition" or in some other arrangement. It is much easier today to break up a marriage and have alternative arrangements for the children's maintenance. Briefly, it would be no exaggeration to say that many people today can live exactly as they wish, with far fewer financial and cultural restrictions than in the past.[23] This description should lead to the conclusion that there are far fewer miserable people; however, research points clearly to the opposite. There is a dramatic rise in the number of cases of clinical depression. In the United States, for example, it is estimated that there are ten times more cases of depression than at the beginning of the twentieth century.[24] Precisely the proliferation of objective possibilities, the growth in freedom of choice, gives more potential space to leaders as "managers of meaning."[25] Leaders are expected to provide answers to psychological situations that stem from disorientation arising paradoxically out of the multiplicity of choices. Management of meaning has different foci at different levels of leadership. At the political level, the focus is more on issues such as national identity. Examples of relations formed around this focus appeared in this book. At the organizational level, the focus can be on the meaning of tasks or ways of achieving more self fulfillment in organizational settings.[26] One way or another, it seems to me that more is expected of leaders today in the psychological sense. The expectations relate more to the "self" of the followers than in the past, when the relations were largely characterized by formal authority and asymmetrical control of resources of power.

In conclusion, it appears that many of the conventional notions are not necessarily correct with regard to leadership in general and transformational leadership in particular. One such conventional notion is the view of the transformational leader's personality as a synthesis of a prophet and a priest. Prophets are those who know how to describe ideas, to depict the future, and foretell what will happen if certain conditions are fulfilled. The priest is the opposite of the prophet; he is a practical person who deals with the "how" – with everyday practice. Leaders are defined in literature – mistakenly, I believe – mainly in these two categories (phrased in various ways). For example, there is literature that describes leaders in terms of vision. The outstanding leaders are visionaries with foresight that enables them to see beyond the horizon visible to most "ordinary" people.[27] On the other hand, there is literature that describes leaders as outstanding doers, as people who make things happen.[28] Transformational leaders are described in some of the literature as a rare combination of prophet and priest, of a man of ideas who is a superb doer, namely, a synthesis of the "what" and the "how," a man of vision who also knows how to implement his ideas perfectly. This view focuses again on the leader himself. In this book we saw leaders who were indeed men of vision, some of them weaker in the practical aspects (Gandhi), whereas others were very strong in the practical aspects and perhaps less in vision (Franklin Roosevelt). Nevertheless, they left their stamp, and this would not have happened without the two elements. A man of vision without practical expression is a prophet, an adviser, or just a prattler. A doer without vision, without a broad view, is a craftsman, a pragmatic manager. However, transformational leaders are not necessarily a synthesis in terms of personality. They have the rare ability to create a "spirit" that combines these two elements in the people around them, a spirit that is oriented towards a better future and at the same time brings out the best in people, inspiring them to use their talents and abilities to the best. These leaders are above all facilitators of the talents, desires, and need for expression of many people. Not always do they do this consciously, but their presence causes people to do their best and demonstrate the more optimistic sides of their personality. They cause people to want not only to **do** more but to **be** more! The analyses and examples presented in this book indicate that leadership literature, especially the more popular literature, places more weight on leaders' rhetoric, frequently quoting the speeches or sayings by transformational leaders. I agree that rhetoric can be important, but it is certainly not the most important element. History shows examples of brilliant rhetoricians who did not excel as leaders, and many examples of the reverse, people whose rhetoric left much to be desired but whose acceptance as outstanding leaders was beyond question. Harry Truman and Yitzhak Rabin are two of the better known examples of this as leaders in the national sphere. But there are many examples in the sphere of leadership in organizations. Most of the examples of leaders cited in this book did not stand out for their rhetorical ability, but they radiated that special spirit by less verbal channels: by their decisions, their typical behaviors, their methods of selective reward and recognition, their lifestyle, and their endless dedication and fervor projected authentically, sometimes uncompromisingly. Enthusiasm and determination are hard to imitate but are certainly infectious. Indirect evidence of their determination can be found precisely in the private lives of some of these outstanding leaders. Herzl was entirely devoted to leading the struggle, there was no room for a private life, hardly any room for his family, and in fact, his wife was miserable. "I am married to the struggle," he used to say (it is interesting that Yasser Arafat, who married only when he reached his sixties, used a similar argument). Mandela separated from his first wife, Evelyn, because he was "married to the political struggle" and had no time or attention to give to his family. And his second wife, Winnie, who was herself involved in politics, wrote in her memoirs: "We never had any life that I can remember as family life, the life of a young bride sitting at ease with her husband. It was never possible to separate Nelson Mandela from the people: the struggle, the nation, came first."[29] Yanush Korchak, the great transformational educator, devoted his whole life to the children in the home where he worked, and did not raise a family of his own. His going with the children to the gas chambers was an expression of his whole way of life: he lived and died with and for the children. This kind of description is not unique, it is intertwined in the lives of many transformational leaders. As we have seen, enthusiasm is infectious. A superficial view of this fervor, this sense of mission, may see only the personal sacrifices it demands, but as I understand it, it is not really a question of choice. Most of these people could not have chosen otherwise. As I remarked elsewhere in this book, an analogy to this kind of ardor and dedication may only be found in the creative arts, such as literature, music, painting, sculpture, and acting. Among great artists, as among great leaders, it is not a question of choice, giving up the "mission" is like denying the libido – denying life energy. Greatness, therefore, is perhaps an imperative of destiny, and the fervor radiated by it (in circumstances that were described in this book as necessary conditions) becomes a flame or a spirit sweeping people along with it.

Some readers may perhaps remember that in the introductory chapter I referred to the way in which Ben Gurion was described (by journalist Uri Avnery) as the figure who created all the drama of the establishment of the state of Israel by the force of his determination and his exclusive leadership. I will close the circle by referring to the example with which I opened. According to the analyses that I have presented here in attempting to create a more integrative frame for understanding the growth and activity of leaders, it seems to me that it would be right to say that everything said by Uri Avnery and others about Ben Gurion is true. The man was determined, motivated by the fervor of a historic mission, with great foresight, and so forth. But all these qualities, in my view, would not have found expression without the historical timing of the circumstances and the psychological and social meanings derived from them. In this case, the circumstances were the growth of an uncompromising need to find a political solution for the Jews, which became more imperative after World War II. Psychologically, the public yearning focused on this urgent need, which became embodied in the person of Ben Gurion at this specific time. It was only this conjunction of circumstances and meanings that gave rise to Ben Gurion's special relationship with the public, a relationship characterized by the symbolic and developmental elements described in this book as elements of transformational leadership. This is the psychological basis for being a transformational leader and it cannot be identified without understanding the context, namely, the relationship existing between the leader and the followers in certain circumstances. The book attempts to illustrate this point. This does not mean that transformational leadership is simply the fruit of a historic meeting between people and circumstances, creating, in the more outstanding cases, a historic drama. Such cases, as I have shown, illustrate more strikingly how the leader is the focus of the desires of the collective, or the personification of the hunger for change, but by no means does this mean that the transformational leader is entirely a product of circumstances. It is certainly not my intention to argue that the entire story of transformational leadership is purely circumstantial!

Leaders' transformative effects stem from, among other things, their ability to exploit the circumstances to the full. Leaders like Gandhi, Lenin, and Roosevelt are salient examples of this. They were able to analyze the circumstances more accurately than others, and this ability enabled them not only to make use of the circumstances to introduce change, as transformational leaders do, but also to create new circumstances and other needs, which might never have come into existence without their intervention. To sum up: on the big question of relations between the leader and the circumstances, the leaders clearly carry great weight in creating new circumstances, but it is important to understand the conditions of their growth and position. Only on this basis can they change or create new circumstances. It seems to me that this type of leader is more rare at the political level, but many outstanding examples may be found in organizations, in education, and in the mundane life of a community.

Notes

Chapter 1. Introduction: What is Leadership?

1. Burns, J.M. (1978). *Leadership*. New York: Harper and Row (p. 473).
2. Thousands of studies on leadership have been collected in books and articles of various kinds. The two best-known handbooks in leadership literature are those of Stogdill and of Bass, which is based to a large extent on the previous work by Stogdill. See Stogdill, R.M. (1974). *Handbook of Leadership Research. A Survey of Theory and Research*. Riverside, NJ: Free Press. See also Bass, B.M. (1990). *Bass & Stogdill's Handbook of Leadership: Theory, Research and Management Application*. New York: Free Press.
3. Leaders' behaviors that generate various effects in terms of motivation and achievements are presented, among others, by Bass, B.M. & Avolio, B.J. (1990). The implications of transactional and transformational leadership for individual, team and organizational development. In R.W. Woodman & W.A. Passmore (eds.), *Research in Organizational Change and Development*. Greenwich, CT: JAI Press (pp. 1–51).
4. Vroom, V. & Yetton, P.W. (1973). *Leadership and Decision Making*. Pittsburgh: University of Pittsburgh Press.
5. Reeves, R. (1995). John F. Kennedy. In R.A. Wilson (ed.), *Character Above All*. New York: Simon & Schuster (pp. 100–22).
6. Lord, R.G. & Maher, K.J. (1993). *Leadership and Information Processing: Linking Perceptions and Performance*. London: Routledge.
7. Kets De Vries, M.F.R. (1989). *Prisoners of Leadership*. New York: John Wiley & Sons.
8. Emile Durkheim wrote of the leader as a personal expression of a broader social group. See Durkheim, E. (1973). The dualism of human nature and its

social conditions. In R. Bellan (ed.), *Emile Durkheim on Morality and Society*. Chicago: University of Chicago Press (pp. 84–117).

9. Sociologist Edward Shills's well-known distinction between "center" and "periphery" refers to these terms in their symbolic sense. That is to say, there are people who are perceived by many others as more representative of the symbolic center of a given society. See Shills, E. (1965). Charisma, order, status. *American Sociological Review*, 30: 199–213.

10. House, R.J. & Adytia, R.N. (1997). The social scientific study of leadership: Quo vadis? *Journal of Management*, 23, 3: 409–72.

11. Many examples of models and studies that have universal value in the sense that they permit forms of cross-cultural comparative research, or rather enable the research planning to include diverse contexts, can be found in the area of attribution. This may be the reason for the outstanding growth of attribution studies in social psychology. One such example from attribution studies is Ross, L., Amebile, T.M. & Steinmatz, J.L. (1977). Social roles, social controls, and biases in social perception processes. *Journal of Personality and Social Psychology*, 35: 485–94.

12. Langer, S.K. (1967). *Mind: An Essay on Human Feeling* (vol. 1). Baltimore, MD: Johns Hopkins University Press (p. 23). Susan Langer argues that: "The entire realm of psychology – including the conceptualizations, operations, the rationality, the knowledge, are simply, offshoots of emotion" (p. 23). The basic claim derives from an evolutionary argument. Emotions are common to all living creatures and have an adaptive function. There is also phylogenetic support for this, related to the structure of the brain. For example, the limbic system, which controls emotions, existed before the development of language, and the infant knows how to express emotions by crying and smiling before he knows how to speak. The argument of adaptivity is also found in leadership literature. For example, see Ronald Heifetz's opinion on the function of leadership in Heifetz, R.H. (1994). *Leadership Without Easy Answers*. Cambridge, Mass: Harvard University.

13. Zajonc's paper is, in fact, a review of the research literature on "cognition versus emotion", and the conclusion he reaches is that emotions create information through separate systems from those that create cognitive information. The practical meaning of this argument is that not only is emotion not a post-cognitive phenomenon, but that it functions separately. See Zajonc, R.B. (1980). Feeling and thinking, preferences need no inferences. *American Psychologist*, 35, 2: 151–175.

14. Emrich et al., using indexes of emotionality derived from studies that examined the emotionality of words and expressions, conducted a comparative analysis of leaders' speeches. See Emrich, C.G., Brower, H.H., Feldman, J.M. et al. (2001). Images in words: Presidential rhetoric, charisma and greatness. *Administrative Science Quarterly*, 46, 3: 527.

15. A literary review on intercultural differences relating to the discussion on leaders appears in an article by Dorfman. See Dorfman, P. (1996). International

and cross-culture leadership. In B.J. Punnett & O.C. Shenkar (eds.), *Handbook of International Management Research*. Oxford: Blackwell (pp. 267–349).

16. See Dorfman, *ibid*.

17. Grauman, C.F. & Moscovici, S. (1986). *Changing Conceptions of Leadership*. New York: Springer-Verlag (pp. 241–2).

18. Smith, P.B., Misumi, J., Tayeb, M., Peterson, M.F. & Bond, M. (1989). On the generality of leadership style measures across cultures. *Journal of Occupational Psychology*, 62: 97–109.

19. Bass, B.M. (1985). *Leadership and Performance Beyond Expectations*. New York: Free Press.

20. Kanungo, R.N. & Mendonca, M. (1996). *Ethical Dimensions in Leadership*. Beverly Hills, CA: Sage Publications.

21. Extensive discussions on the romanticization existing in relating to leaders are presented, for example, by Meindl, J.R., Ehrlich, S.B. & Dukerich, J.M. (1985). The romance of leadership. *Administrative Science Quarterly*, 30: 78–102. See also Meindl, J.R. (1995). The romance of leadership as follower-centric theory: A social construction approach. *Leadership Quarterly*, 6: 329–41.

22. Wilson, R.A., ed. (1995). *Character Above All*. New York: Simon & Schuster (p. x).

23. Popper, M. (2002). Salient biases in discussion and research on leadership. In K. Parry & J. Meindl (eds.), *Grounding Leadership Theory and Research: Findings and Implications*. Greenwich, CT: Information Age Publishing (pp. 1–20).

24. Shamir, B., House, R.J. & Arthur, M.B. (1993). The motivational effects of charismatic leadership: A self concept based theory. *Organizational Science*, 4: 577–93.

25. Bernard Bass refers a great deal to the idea of the followers acting above and beyond as a criterion for evaluating leaders' influence. See Bass, B.M. (1985). *Leadership and Performance beyond Expectations*. New York: Free Press (p. x)

26. Maslow, A. (1970). *Motivation and Personality*. New York: Harper & Row.

27. Burns, J.M. (1978). *Leadership*. New York: Harper & Row (p. x).

28. Alderfer, C.P. (1972). *Existence, Relatedness and Growth*. New York: Free Press.

29. Pillai, R. (1996). Crisis and the emergence of charismatic leadership in groups: An experimental investigation. *Journal of Applied Social Psychology*, 26: 543–62.

30. Durkheim, E. (1973). The dualism of human nature and its social conditions. In R. Bellan (ed.), *Emile Durkheim on Morality and Society*. Chicago: University of Chicago Press (pp. xx–xx).

31. Stryker, S. (1980). *Symbolic Interactionism – A Social Structural Version*. Menlo Park, CA: Benjamin Cummings.

32. McClelland, D.C. (1975). *Power: The Inner Experience*. New York: Irvington.
33. Popper, M. (2001). *Hypnotic Leadership: Leaders, Followers, and the Loss of Self*. Westport, CT: Praeger.
34. Storr, A. (1972). *The Dynamics of Creation*. London: Secker & Warburg.
35. Bowlby, J. (1988). *A Secure Base: Clinical Applications of Attachment Theory*. London: Routledge.
36. Schwartz, B. (2000). *Abraham Lincoln. Forge of National Memory*. Chicago: University of Chicago Press.
37. Burns, J.M. & Dun, S. (2001). *The Three Roosevelts: Patrician Leaders Who Transformed America*. New York: Atlantic Monthly Press (p. x).
38. Goodwin, D.K. (1995). Franklin Roosevelt 1933–1945. In R.A. Wilson (ed.), *Character Above All: Ten Presidents from FDR to George Bush*. New York: Simon and Schuster (pp. 13–38).
39. See Chadha, Y. (1997). *Gandhi: A Life*. New York: John Wiley & Sons (p. x); Sampson, A. (1999). *Mandela*. London: Harper and Collins and Ayalon, A. (1976). *Herzl*. Tel Aviv: Am Oved (in Hebrew).
40. Popper, M. & Mayseless, O. Back to basics (2003). Applying parental notions to transformational leadership. *Leadership Quarterly*, 14, 41–65. See also Shamir, B., House, R.J. & Arthur, M.B. (1993). The motivational effects of charismatic leadership: A self concept based theory. *Organizational Science*, 4: 577–93.
41. Erikson, E.H. (1969). *Gandhi's Truth: On the Origins of Militant Non-violence*. New York: Norton (p. x).
42. Burns, J.M. (1978). *Leadership*. New York: Harper and Row.
43. Westphal, M. (1992). *Hegel, Freedom and Modernity*. New York: State University of New York Press.

Chapter 2. A Bird's-eye View of Leadership

1. Charles Lindholm, a researcher from Harvard University, dealt with the emotional effect of leaders, comparing leadership to romantic relations. In an article entitled "Lovers and leaders," he argues that emotional processes characteristic of falling in love resemble the process of followers' attachment to a charismatic leader. Lindholm, C. (1988). Lovers and leaders. *Social Science Information*, 16: 227–246.
2. Meindl et al., who surveyed dozens of titles of articles and books on leadership, pointed out the frequent use of what they refer to as "mystic" terms. Meindl, J.R., Ehrlich, S.B. & Dukerich, J.M. (1985). The romance of leadership. *Administrative Science Quarterly*, 30: 78–102.
3. Plato. (1973). *The Collected Dialogues of Plato*. New Jersey: Princeton University Press.
4. Carlyle, T. (1907). *On Heroes, Hero-Worship and the Heroic in History* (written in 1841). Boston: Houghton Mifflin.
5. Machiavelli, N. (1985). *The Prince*. Chicago: University of Chicago Press.

6. Terman, L.M. (1904). A preliminary study of the psychology of leadership. In R.M. Stogdill (ed.), *Handbook of Leadership Research: A Survey of Theory and Research*. Riverside Drive, N.J.: Free Press. pp. 38–61. Another comprehensive review of studies in leadership may be found in Bass, B.M. (1990). *Bass & Stogdill's Handbook of Leadership: Theory, Research and Management Applications*. New York: Free Press.

7. Stogdill, R.M. (1948). Personal factors associated with leadership: A survey of the literature. *Journal of Psychology*, 25: 37–71.

8. Burns, J.M. (1978). *Leadership*. New York: Harper & Row.

9. Bass, B.M. (1985). *Leadership and Performance beyond Expectations*. New York: Free Press.

10. Heifetz, R.H. (1994). *Leadership Without Easy Answers*. Cambridge, Mass: Harvard University Press.

11. Some theoretical articles on the psychological distinction between positive and negative leaders have been published, notably the following: See House, R.J. & Howell, J.M. (1992). Personality and charismatic leadership. *Leadership Quarterly*, 3, 2: 81–108. See also Howell, J.M. (1988). Two faces of charisma: Socialized and personalized leadership in organizations. In A.J. Conger & K.N. Kanungoo (eds.), *Charismatic Leadership and the Elusive Factor in Organizational Effectiveness*. San Francisco: Jossey Bass. pp. 213–236. For an empirical study on the distinction between socialized and personalized leaders, see Popper, M. (2002). Narcissism and attachment patterns of personalized and socialized charismatic leaders. *Journal of Social and Personal Relations*, 19, 6: 796–808.

12. Some important studies on the internal representations that influence the behaviors of individuals from childhood to maturity were presented by Bowlby, J. (1988). *A Secure Base: Clinical Applications of Attachment Theory*. London: Routledge. See also Hazan, C. & Shaver, P. (1987). Romantic love conceptualized as an attachment process. *Journal of Personality and Social Psychology*, 52: 511–524. In the last few years, research on the emotions has developed considerably. For example, studies on "emotional intelligence" have also been conducted in the context of leadership. See, for example, Goleman, D. (1995). *Emotional Intelligence*. New York: Bantam Books. See also Goleman, D. (1998). *Working with Emotional Intelligence*. New York: Bantam Books and Salovay, P. & Mayer, J.D. (1990). Emotional intelligence. *Imagination, Cognition and Personality*, 9, 3: 185–211.

13. An example of this kind of study is Popper, M., Amit, K., Gal, R., et al. (2004). The capacity to lead: Major psychological differences between "leaders" and "non-leaders." *Military Psychology*, 16, 4, pp. 245–63.

14. See, for example: Avolio, B.J., & Gibbons, T.C. (1988). developing transformational leaders: A life span approach. In Conger, J.A. & Kanungo, R.N. (Eds.), *Charismatic Leadership: The Elusive Factor of Organizational Effectiveness* (pp. 276–308). San Francisco, CA: Jossey-Bass. Avolio, B. (1999). *Full Leadership Development*. London: Sage Publications. Judge, A., Bono,

J. E. (2000). Five factor model of personality and transformational leadership *Journal of Applied Psychology, 85*, 751–765. Day, D.V. (2000) Leadership Development: A review in context. *Leadership Quarterly*, 11, 581–613

15. Shaf, A. (1950). *Marxism – Leninism*. Merhavia (p. 90) (in Hebrew). Sowell, T. (1985). *Marxism: Philosophy and Economics*. New York: Morrow.

16. Some experimental studies, as well as sociological and historical reviews, point to the circumstantial component (especially a crisis situation) as decisive in the emergence of leaders. An example is Pillai, R. (1996). Crisis and the emergence of charismatic leadership in groups: An experimental investigation. *Journal of Applied Social Psychology*, 26: 543. Another example is Herzber, J.O. (1940). Crises and dictatorships. *American Sociological Review*, 5: 157–160.

17. Reddin, W.J. (1970). *Managerial Effectiveness*. New York: McGraw-Hill.

18. Fiedler, F.F. (1967). *A Theory of Leadership Effectiveness*. New York: McGraw-Hill.

19. Reddin, W.J. (1967). The 3-D management style theory. *Training and Developmental Journal*, April 8–17.

20. Meindl, J.R. (1995). The romance of leadership as follower-centric theory: A social construction approach. *Leadership Quarterly*, 6: 329–341.

21. Weber, M. (1974, first publication 1922) *From Max Weber: Essays in Sociology*. H. Gerth & C. Wright Mills (eds). New York: Oxford University Press (pp. 358–359).

22. Kershaw, I. (1989). *Hitler, 1889–1936: Hubris*. London: The Penguin Press (p. 10).

23. An illustration of leadership studies based on cognitive psychological theories is presented in the works of Conger and Kanungo and of Meindl et al. The former show how behavioral clues – certain forms of behavior – create stronger attribution of leadership. The latter show how images of leadership are formed from information read in newspapers. See Conger, J.A. & Kanungo, R.N. (1987). Toward a behavioral theory of charismatic leadership in organizational settings. *Academy of Management Review*, 12: 637–47. See also Meindl, J.R., Erlich, S.B. & Dukerich, J.M. (1985). The romance of leadership. *Administrative Science Quarterly*, 30: 78–102.

24. Kets de Vries wrote extensively on leadership from a psychological viewpoint that emphasizes parallel processes between parent-child relations and leader-follower relations. See Kets de Vries, M.F.R. (1989). *Prisoners of Leadership*. New York: John Wiley & Sons.

25. Post, J.M. (1986). Narcissism and the charismatic leader-follower relationship. *Political Psychology*, 7, 4: 675–87.

26. The Dutch scholar, Geert Hofstede, has dealt extensively with the comparison of national cultures. In his research, based also on previous attempts by sociologists to deal with national character, he found four dimensions for comparison of nations (in later studies he added another dimension). These dimensions are "power distance," which expresses the attitude toward authority,

masculinity-femininity, individualism-collectivism, and tolerance of uncertainty. See Hofstede, G. (1997). *Cultures and Organizations. The Software of the Mind*. New York: McGraw-Hill.

Chapter 3. Analysis of the Main Perspectives on Leadership

1. Uri Avneri, "A unique figure in his time" *Ma'ariv* Weekend Supplement, April 29, 1998, pp. 56–63 (in Hebrew).
2. On Thomas Carlyle's approach, see: Carlyle, T. (1907). *On Heroes, Hero-Worship and the Heroic in History* (written in 1841). Boston: Houghton Mifflin.
3. Malthus and his influence are discussed in a book by Barry Schwartz: Schwartz, B. (1986). *The Battle for Human Nature*. New York: Norton.
4. Marx, K. & Engels, F. (1968). *The Communist Manifesto*. New York: Modern Reader Paperbacks.
5. A comprehensive survey of the development of personality theories, emphasizing the changes in relation to Freud's theory can be found in Maddi, S.R. (1996). *Personality Theories: A Comparative Analysis*. New York: Brooks/Cole Publishing.
6. James MacGregor Burns, an eminent writer on leadership and a presidential scholar, who studied in depth the leadership of some of the presidents of the United States. His book, *Leadership*, published in 1978 by Harper and Row, is one of the most cited references in leadership literature.
7. For a review of the various definitions of leadership and of "influence" as a central theme in most conceptual frameworks dealing with leadership, see Rost, J.C. (1991). *Leadership for the Twenty-First Century*. New York: Praeger.
8. Kotter wrote articles and books on the distinctive characteristics of the leadership phenomenon. See, for example, Kotter, J. (1990). What do leaders really do? *Harvard Business Review*, May–June: 103–11. See also Kotter, J. (1990). *The Leadership Factor*. New York: The Free Press.
9. Willner, in her book about charismatic leaders in the political sphere, analyzes the secret of their success: Willner, A.R. (1984). *The Spellbinders: Charismatic Political Leaders*. New Haven CT: Yale University Press.
10. Larsen, A. (1968). *The President Nobody Knew*. New York: Popular Library.
11. Explanations and illustrations from research on the fundamental attribution error may be found in the following article: Ross, L., Amabile, T.M., & Steinmetz, J.L. (1977). Social roles, social controls, and biases in social perception processes. *Journal of Personality and Social Psychology*, 35: 485–494.
12. Examples of this appear in: Calder, J.B. (1977). An attribution theory of leadership. In: Staw, B.M. & R., Salacick (eds), *New Directions in Organizational Behavior*. Chicago: St. Clair, pp. 179–204.
13. Kosinski, J. (1972). *Being There*. New York: Bantam Books.

14. On the process of attribution of leadership behaviors, see Conger, J.A. & Kanungo, R.N. (1987). Toward a behavior theory of charismatic leadership in organizational settings. *Academy of Management Review*, 12: 637–47.

15. The following articles deal with the romanticization of leadership and the phenomenon of social contagion: Meindl, J.R., Ehrlich, S.B., & Dukerich, J.M. (1985). The romance of leadership. *Administrative Science Quarterly*, 30: 78–102 and Meindl, J.R. (1990). On leadership: An alternative to conventional wisdom. *Research in Organizational Behavior*, 12: 159–203.

16. The effect of distance on the followers' perceptions is discussed in Shamir, B. (1995). Social distance and charisma. Theoretical notes and explanatory study. *Leadership Quarterly*, 1: 19–48.

17. Popper, M. (2001). *Hypnotic Leadership: Leaders, Followers, and the Loss of Self*. Westport CT: Praeger (Greenwood Publishing Group).

18. On general issues of construction of social reality from a subjective viewpoint, see, for example, the book by Peter Bergman and Thomas Luckman: Berger, P. & Luckman, T. (1996). *The Social Construction of Reality*. Garden City, New York: Doubleday. The specific issue of construction of the figures of leaders from the viewpoint of the observer is discussed by Bobby Calder: Calder, B.J. (1997). An attribution theory of leadership. In B.M. Staw & G.R. Salancik (eds.), *New Directions in Organizational Behavior*. Chicago: St. Clair (pp. 179–204).

19. The sociologists Inkeles and Levinson attempted to identify the reasons for the formation of differences in national character. See Inkeles, A. & Levinson, D.J. (1969). National character: the study of modal personality and sociocultural systems. In: G. Lindsey & E. Aronson (eds.), *The Handbook of Social Psychology* (2nd edition, vol. 4). Reading, MA: Addison-Wesley, pp. 418–506. Geert Hofstede conducted a large comparative study on intercultural differences. See: Hofstede, G. (1997). *Cultures and Organizations: The Software of the Mind*. New York: McGraw-Hill.

20. Hofstede, ibid.

21. Popper, M. (1994). *On Managers as Leaders*. Tel Aviv: Ramot Press, Tel Aviv University (in Hebrew).

22. Gerstner, C.R. & Day, D.V. (1994). Cross-cultural comparison of leadership prototypes. *Leadership Quarterly*, 5: 121–34.

23. Popper, M. & Druyan, N. (2001). Cultural prototypes? Or leaders behaviors? A study on workers' perceptions of leadership in an electronics industry. *Journal of Managerial Psychology*, 16, 7: 549–58.

24. For an explanation and examples of the projection mechanism, see Rycroft, C. (1995). *Dictionary of Psychoanalysis*. London: Penguin Books.

25. On the leader as a father figure, see Freud, S. (1939). *Moses and Monotheism. The Standard Edition of the Complete Psychological Works of Sigmund Freud* (vol. XVIII). London: The Hogarth Press, pp. 109–10.

26. On the need to study the leadership phenomenon through the followers' perceptions, see: Meindl, J.R. (1995). The romance of leadership as follower-

centric theory: A social construction approach. *Leadership Quarterly*, 6: 329–41.

27. Popper, M. (1994). See previous 21. *On Managers as Leaders*.
28. For a discussion on rationality and emotionality in human nature as reflected mainly in the disciplines of philosophy and sociology, see Lindholm, C. (1990). *Charisma*. London: Blackwell.
29. The idea of viewing interpersonal relations through the paradigm of exchange relations was presented by Homans, and spawned a great deal of research in sociology and social psychology dealing with interpersonal relations. See Homans, G.C. (1950). *The Human Group*. New York: Harcourt Brace. See also Homans, G.C. (1962). *Sentiments and Activities: Essays in Social Science*. New York: Free Press.
30. For a discussion on rational motivational assumptions, see Vroom, V. & Yetton, P.W. (1973). *Leadership and Decision Making*. Pittsburgh: University of Pittsburgh Press.
31. In the 1960s and 1970s some models were formulated that explicitly stressed instrumentality in leader-follower relations. This paradigm was expressed mainly in research on leadership in organizations. Typical examples of this thinking are presented in House, R.J. (1971). A path goal theory of leader effectiveness. *Administrative Science Quarterly*, 16: 321–8. Current leadership literature also includes conceptualizations describing leadership, or a certain type of leadership, in terms of transactions. The most salient concept is transactional leadership. See, for example, Bass, B.M. & Avolio, B.J. (1990). The implications of transactional and transformational leadership for individual, team and organizational development. In R.W. Woodman & W.A. Passmore (eds.), *Research in Organizational Change and Development*. Greenwich, CT: JAI Press, 4, pp. 231–72.
32. Some scholars have dealt with the elements of motivation in the context of pro-social behavior, namely behavior oriented towards the general good, sometimes in contrast to the visible logic of self interest, see for example: Frans de Waal (1996). *Good Natured: The Origins of Right and Wrong in Humans and Other Animals*. Cambridge, Mass: Harvard University Press. A discussion on social behaviors known in the literature as prosocial behaviors is presented by Bar-Tal, D. (1976). *Prosocial Behavior*. New York: John Wiley.
33. See, for example, Maslow, A. (1970). *Motivation and Personality*. New York: Harper & Row.
34. See Frankl, V.E. (1963). *Man's Search for Meaning: An Introduction to Logotherapy*. Boston: Beacon Press.
35. The case of Jim Jones is described by Lindholm, C. (1990). *Charisma*. London: Blackwell.
36. For a comprehensive biography of Gandhi, see Chadha, Y. (1997). *Gandhi: A Life*. New York: John Wiley & Sons.
37. Continuing the previous reference to projection, it is defined in Rycroft's psychoanalytical dictionary as "viewing a mental image as objective reality."

Rycroft, C. (1995). *Dictionary of Psychoanalysis*. London: Penguin Books (p. 139). In clinical psychology and psychiatry there are two meanings of projection. One concerns misinterpretations of dreams and fantasies and the other (which is more relevant to the present discussion) refers to the process whereby aspects of the self (impulses and wishes) are imagined to be present in another person.

38. The concept of transference was originally formulated as a central element in the relations between therapist and patient. It is defined in Rycroft's Dictionary of Psychoanalysis as "The process by which a patient displaces on to his analyst ideas, etc., which derive from previous figures in his life" (p. 185). This concept was expanded to include other forms of relationships, such as those with leaders. See the discussion on this in Kets De Vries, M.F.R. (1989). *Prisoners of Leadership*. New York: John Wiley & Sons.

39. A psychological analysis of relationships like that of falling in love appears in: Alberoni, F. (1983). *Falling in Love*. New York: Random House. Singer, I. (1987). *The Nature of Love*. Chicago: University of Chicago Press.

40. Freud, S. (1939). *Moses and Monotheism. Second Edition of the Complete Psychological Works of Sigmund Freud* (vol. XVIII). London: The Hogarth Press (pp. 109–10).

41. A psychological analysis of emotional leader-follower relationships as they existed in a number of extreme cases is presented by Popper, M. (2001). *Hypnotic Leadership*. Westport, CT: Praeger.

42. For Manson's account of himself, see Emmons, R. (1985). *Manson in His Own Words*. New York: Grove Press (p. 24).

43. Interview with an Israeli journalist who visited him in jail. See "I am Charles Manson." Ma'ariv weekend supplement, March 14, 1997 (in Hebrew).

44. Watson, T. (1978). *Will You Die for Me?* New Jersey, Old Tappan: Fleming H. Revell (p. 61).

45. Watson, ibid., p. 72.

46. From: "I am Charles Manson." (See previous Note 43.)

47. From: *Manson in His Own Words*, p. 183 (See previous Note 42).

48. The story of Jim Jones with an analysis of the events that preceded the mass suicide appears in the book: Reiterman, T. & Jacobs, J. (1982). *The Untold Story of the Rev. Jim Jones and his People*. New York: Button. See also Reston, J. (1981). *Our Father Who Art in Hell*. New York: Times Book.

49. The two most prominent scholars who dealt with narcissism are Otto Kernberg and Heinz Kohut. See Kernberg, O. (1982). Narcissism. In: *Introducing Psychoanalytic Theory*. London: Methuen. See also Kohut, H. (1971). *The Analysis of the Self*. New York: International University Press. For the application of theories on narcissism in the study of leadership, see Post, J.M. (1986). Narcissism and the charismatic leader follower relationship. *Political Psychology*, 14: 675–88.

50. See André Maurois' book on Balzac: Maurois, A. (1965). *Prometheus, Balzac's Life*. London: Bodley Head.

51. On art as a therapeutic process, see Storr, A. (1972). *The Dynamics of Creation.* London: Secker and Warburg.

52. See Kohut, previous Note 49. See also Post's article (Note 49), which is based on Kohut's theory on leadership, particularly on leader-follower relations.

53. Psychoanalyst David Aberbach offers a psychodynamic explanation of leader-follower relations based on personal and collective traumas. See Aberbach, D. (1995). Charisma and attachment theory: A cross-disciplinary interpretation. *International Journal of Psychoanalysis*, 76: 845–55.

54. For examples and explanations of regressive leader-follower relations, see Popper (Note 17) previously.

55. On the difference between strong and weak psychological situations, see Mischel, W. (1973). Toward a cognitive social learning conceptualization of personality. *Psychological Review*, 80: 252–83.

56. Franklin Delano Roosevelt's inauguration ceremony is described in Schlesinger, M. Jr. (1958). *The Coming of the New Deal.* Boston: Houghton Mifflin (pp. 1–2).

57. Explanations of Hitler's psychological influence on his path to government are presented by Fest, J. (1974). *Hitler.* New York: Harcourt, Brace, Jovanovich.

58. A review of the link between crisis situations and the rise of outstanding leaders in history is presented by Bernard Bass in his book Bass, B.M. (1985). *Leadership and Performance beyond Expectations.* New York: Free Press.

59. An analysis of the rise of 35 dictators in times of crisis appears in Hertzber, J.O. (1940). *Crisis and Dictatorships. American Sociological Review*, 5: 157–60.

60. For an analysis of the differences between leadership in military and business organizations, see Popper, M. (1996). Leadership in military combat units and business organizations: A comparative psychological analysis. *Journal of Managerial Psychology*, 15: 15–25.

61. See Woodward, who refers, among other things, to the connection between technology and leadership. Woodward, J. (1965). *Industrial Organizations: Theory and Practice.* Oxford: Oxford University Press.

62. See Popper, Note 41 earlier.

63. Micha Popper and Ofra Mayseless compared studies dealing with leader-follower relations with studies on parenting. The findings clearly indicate a similarity in the emotional effects. For instance, both socialized leaders and good parents provide opportunities for and experiences of development, they form relations of trust, and inspire their children/followers with the wish to achieve. See Popper, M. & Mayseless, O. (2003). Back to basics. Applying parenting perspectives to transformational leadership. *Leadership Quarterly*, 14: 41–65.

64. Many theories emphasize the centrality of childhood in the processes of emotional and social development. Two of the most prominent theories in developmental psychology are those of Sigmund Freud and John Bowlby. It was the latter that to a large extent made it possible to conduct empirical studies on the basis of Freud's arguments. See Freud, S. (1920). *A General Introduction*

to Psychoanalysis. American Edition. Garden City (pp. 363–5). See also Bowlby, J. (1969). *Attachment and Loss*: Vol. 1. *Attachment*. New York: Basic Books.

65. See the comprehensive official biography of Nelson Mandela by Anthony Sampson: Sampson, A. (1999). *Mandela*. London: Harper and Row.

66. See Ronald Heifetz's book, which is based on the assumption that the leader's main function is adaptive, and therefore his major role is to supply the primary needs (in Maslow's terms) or to perform survival functions in Darwin's terms. Heifetz, R.H. (1994). *Leadership Without Easy Answers*. Cambridge, Mass: Harvard University Press.

67. See Note 63 previously. The comparison is based on the argument presented in developmental psychological theories (such as those of John Bowlby) that in the absence of a sense of security the child clings to the caring parent, whereas the sense of security frees the child to engage in behaviors marked by more initiative, more discovery, and much more curiosity and readiness to take risks.

68. See Popper & Mayseless, Note 63 previously.

69. See Mayseless, O. & Popper, M. (2005). Leader-follower relations: An attachment perspective (under review). See Kotter, J.P. (1988). *The Leadership Factor*. New York: The Free Press.

70. Sampson, A. *Mandela*, p. 408.

71. Sampson, p. 411.

72. Sampson, p. 412.

73. See Kranz, H. (1959). (ed.). *Abraham Lincoln: A New Portrait*. New York: Freeport (p. 38).

74. Schwartz, B. (2000). *Abraham Lincoln. Forge of National Memory*. Chicago: University of Chicago Press.

75. A study that examined the number of entries on presidents in the Library of Congress found that George Washington was the largest focus of interest until the beginning of the twentieth century. With the passing of time, Abraham Lincoln increasingly became a source of interest and was more quoted, until in 1921 Lincoln's average was 20.7, compared with 6.3 for George Washington. For details, see Schwartz (Note 73).

76. Among the most famous books on the need for meaning as a motivational force are those by Abraham Maslow and Victor Frankl. See, for example, Maslow, A. (1970). *Motivation and Personality*. New York: Harper and Row. See also Frankl, V.E. (1963). *Man's Search for Meaning: An Introduction to Logotherapy*. Boston: Beacon Press.

77. A review of the ideas of John Dewey, Max Weber, Robert Linton, and John Herbert Mead appears in a book by Stryker, S. (1980). *Symbolic Interactionism. A Social Structural Version*. Menlo Park, California: Benjamin Cummings.

78. See Schwartz, Note 74.

79. Schein, E. (1985). *Organizational Culture and Leadership*. San Francisco: Jossey Bass.

80. Chadha, Y. (1997). *Gandhi: A Life*. New York: John Wiley & Sons.
81. Shamir, B., House, R.J., & Arthur, M.B. (1993). The motivational effects of charismatic leadership: A self concept based theory. *Organizational Science*, 4: 577–93.
82. Macintyre, A. (1981). *After Virtue: A Study in Moral Theory*. London: Duckworth (p. 201).
83. Shils, E. (1965). Charisma, order, status. *American Sociological Review*, 30: 199–213.
84. See Shamir et al., Note 81.
85. Kleinberg, A. (2000). *Fra Ginepro's Leg of Pork: Christian Saints' Stories and their Cultural Roles*. Tel Aviv: Zmora Bitan (p. 14) (in Hebrew).
86. Quoted from Kleinberg's book, Note 85, p. 15.
87. Klein, M. (1948). *Contribution to Psychoanalysis*. London: Hogarth Press.
88. Quoted from David Ben Gurion's memoirs. In Ohana, D. (2003). *From Messianism to Statism. Ben Gurion and the Intellectuals*. Be'er Sheva: Ben Gurion University Press (p. 37) (in Hebrew).
89. Popper, M. (2001). *Hypnotic Leadership: Leaders, Followers, and the Loss of Self*. Westport, CT: Praeger.

Chapter 4. Transformational Leadership

1. Eilon, A. (1976). *Herzl*. Tel Aviv: Am Oved Publishers, p. 266 (in Hebrew).
2. Eilon, 1976, p. 267.
3. Eilon, 1976, p. 268.
4. Meindl and associates argue that there are social processes whereby romantic images of leaders are formed. These processes occur among the followers and are not initiated by the leader. The following articles deal with this radical claim, both at the theoretical and empirical level: Meindl, J.R., Erlich, S.B. & Dukerich, J.M. (1985). The romance of leadership. *Administrative Science Quarterly*, 30: 78–102. Meindl, J.R. (1990). On leadership: An alternative to conventional wisdom. *Research in Organizational Behavior*, 12: 159–203. Meindl, J.R. (1995). The romance of leadership as follower-centric theory: A social construction approach. *Leadership Quarterly*, 6: 329–41.
5. Fest, J. (1974). *Hitler*. New York: Harcourt Brace.
6. Lindholm, C. (1990). *Charisma*. London: Blackwell.
7. Eilon, 1976, p. 233.
8. Eilon, 1976, p. 234.
9. Of the various biographies of Nelson Mandela, the one by Anthony Sampson was written with Mandela's full cooperation: Sampson, A. (1999). *Mandela*. London: Harper & Collins (p. 412).
10. Schreck, N. (ed.) (1988). *The Manson File*. New York: Amok Press (p. 48).
11. Popper, M. (2001). *Hypnotic Leadership: Leaders, Followers and the Loss of Self*. Westport CT: Praeger.
12. Reiterman, T. & Jacobs, J. (1982). *Raven: the Untold Story of the Rev. Jim Jones and his People*. New York: Button, p. 45.

13. Moore, R. (1986). *The Jonestown Letters: Correspondence of the More Family, 1970–1985*. Lewiston, MN: Edwin Mellen Press.

14. For a theoretical discussion on the concept of empowerment in various disciplines, see: Sadan, E. (1997). *Empowerment and Community Planning*. Tel Aviv: Hakibbutz Hameuchad publishers (in Hebrew). For a discussion on empowerment as a psychological concept at the level of the individual, see Conger and Kanungo: Conger, J.A. & Kanungo, R.N. (1988). The empowerment process: Integration and practice. *Academy of Management Review*, 13: 471–82. A series of studies that present the sources of empowerment and its psychological and behavioral expressions, as well as the relations between management and empowerment,was presented by Spreitzer and colleagues: Spreitzer, G.M. (1995). Psychological empowerment in the workplace. Dimensions, measurement and validation. *Academy of Management Journal*, 38, 5: 1442–65. See also Spreitzer, G.M., De Janasz, S.C. & Quinn, R.E. (1999). Empowered to lead: The role of psychological empowerment in leadership. *Journal of Organizational Behavior*, 20. 4: 511–26.

15. These themes, taken from existential philosophy, were "translated psychologically" by well-known psychologists such as Viktor Frankl and Carl Rogers. See E Sadan, *Empowerment and Community Planning*, p. 12.

16. There are different types of empowerment. The discussion in this book refers to psychological empowerment, which is expressed in enhanced self acceptance and self confidence, social and political understanding, and personal ability to take a meaningful part in decision making processes concerning one's fate. The empowerment process mainly leads to an internal change in individuals' belief in their ability to solve their problems (Spreitzer, G.M., De Janasz, S.C. & Quinn, R.E., 1999, Note 14).

17. The term self efficacy relates to the individual's belief in his/her ability to succeed in specific areas. The many studies conducted to locate the factors that lead to self efficacy found that the most important factor is the experience of success. The more an individual experiences success in a certain area the more his self efficacy grows in that area. The research findings showed that it is possible to generate changes in self efficacy. The scholar who formulated the concept and made it a central one in processes such as empowerment is Albert Bandura. See: Bandura, A. (ed.) (1995). *Self Efficacy in Changing Societies*. New York, NY: Cambridge University Press.

18. Presidential scholar Doris Goodwin wrote a great deal about President Roosevelt's contribution during the Depression and the period leading up to World War II. Goodwin mainly studied the periods of Franklin Delano Roosevelt and Lyndon Johnson. An article evaluating Roosevelt's functioning appeared in a collection of papers edited by Wilson. Goodwin, D.K. (1995). Franklin Roosevelt 1933–1945. In R.A. Wilson (ed.), *Character Above All: Ten Presidents from FDR to George Bush*. New York: Simon & Schuster (pp. 13–30).

19. See Goodwin, 1995, p. 17.

20. Burns, J.M. & Dun, S. (2001). *The Three Roosevelts: Patrician Leaders who Transformed America*. New York: Atlantic Monthly Press.
21. Maslow, A. (1970). *Motivation and Personality*. New York: Harper & Row.
22. Burns, J.M. (1978). *Leadership*. New York: Harper & Row.
23. Bass, B.M. (1985). *Leadership and Performance beyond Expectations*. New York: Free Press, p. 15.
24. A discussion on transformational leaders' influence on ideological and moral aspects appears in Burns' book cited above, pp. 5–74.
25. Piaget, J. (1999). *The Moral Judgement of the Child*. London: Routledge.
26. Kohlberg's contribution, which focuses on the cognitive aspects of moral development, laid the conceptual foundation for the extensive research that was conducted on the subject. Kohlberg, L. (1963). Moral development and identification. In H.W. Stevenson (ed.), *Child Psychology*. Chicago: Chicago University Press (pp. 232–77). See also Kohlberg, L. (1969). Stages and sequences: The cognitive developmental approach to socialization. In D. Goslin (ed.), *Handbook of Socialization Theory and Research*. Chicago, Ill: Rand McNally, pp. 347–480.
27. Kohlberg's model for the development of moral judgment was based on long-range research in which he traced the development of seventy-five boys aged ten to twelve over a period of ten years. Kohlberg presented his subjects with stories whose heroes faced a moral dilemma and asked them questions about this dilemma. In his analysis, Kohlberg did not relate to the actual judgment (whether the protagonist had acted rightly or not), but to the arguments used by the subjects in explaining their judgment. For example, the most famous dilemma that Kohlberg presented to his subjects was that of Heintz: In Europe a woman was dying of a severe illness, the doctors informed her husband Heintz that only one medicine could save her life. This medicine had been invented by a pharmacist who lived in the same town. Preparation of a minute amount of the drug cost the pharmacist $200 but he was asking $2000 for it. Heintz tried to borrow the money from his friends, but only managed to raise half of the sum. So he went to the pharmacist, told him that his wife was dying and asked him to sell him the medicine at half the price, saying that he would pay the rest later. No, said the pharmacist, I will not. I invented this medicine and I intend to profit from it. At night Heintz broke into the pharmacy and stole the drug. The subjects were asked whether Heinz should have broken into the pharmacy. Was it a good or a bad act? They were asked to give reasons for their answers. Most of the research consisted of identifying the patterns of argumentation at different ages of the subjects. Based on this analysis, Kohlberg formulated his model.
28. Colby, A., Kohlberg, L., Gibbs, J., et al. (1983). A longitudinal study of moral judgment. *Monographs of the Society for Research in Child Development*, 48 (1–2), serial no. 200.
29. Colby et al., 1983.
30. Colby et al., 1983.

31. The monumental works of Piaget and Kohlberg studied cognitive aspects of moral development. Hoffman was one of the pioneers who focused on the study of affective aspects of pro-social behavior. See, for example: Hoffman, M.L. (2000). Empathy and Moral Development: Implications for Caring and Justice. Cambridge: Cambridge University Press.

32. One of the tests of transformational leadership according to Bernard Bass's well-known book is "behavior above and beyond," that is to say, behavior that expresses endeavor and contribution beyond the conventional in a given normative environment. See: Bass, B.M. (1985). Leadership and Performance beyond Expectations. New York: Free Press.

33. On altruistic behaviors of animals, see: France de Waal (1996). Good Natured: the Origins of Right and Wrong in Humans and Other Animals. Harvard University Press.

34. For a critical historical discussion of assumptions underlying theories dealing with human nature, see Barry Schwartz: Schwartz, B. (1986). The Battle for Human Nature. Science, Morality and Modern Life. New York: Norton.

35. Frankl, V.E. *Man's Search for Meaning: An Introduction to Logotherapy.* Boston: Beacon Press.

36. See Hoffman, (2000).

37. Feigenson, N. (1997). Sympathy and legal judgment. *Tennessee Law Review*, 65: 1–78.

38. The processes of stripping empathy and similar feelings are described by Lifton as well as by Schein et al in studies conducted among prisoners. See: Lifton, R.J. (1961). Thought Reform and the Psychology of Totalism. New York: Norton. Schein, E., Schnier, I. & Barker, C.H. (1961). Coercive Persuasion. A Socio-psychological Analysis of the "Brainwashing" of American Civilian Prisoners by Chinese Communities. New York: Norton.

39. Examples of the processes of dehumanization that certain leaders create are presented by Micha Popper in the book: Popper, M. (2001). Hypnotic Leadership: Leaders, Followers and the Loss of Self. Westport, CT: Praeger.

40. Sampson, 1999, p. 528.

41. TRC Report, vol. 1, p. 126.

42. These words of Gillian Slovo, the daughter of one of the prominent leaders of the resistance in South Africa, reflected the attitude of those who were in favor of the TRC. See: Slovo, Gillian (1998). Guardian, October 11.

43. Graca Marcel, in an interview with Nelson Mandela's official biographer, Anthony Sampson, February 22, 1998.

44. Chadha, Y. (1997). *Gandhi: A Life.* New York: John Wiley & Sons (p. 282).

45. Shamir, B. (1995). Social distance and charisma. Theoretical notes and explanatory study. *Leadership Quarterly*, 1: 19–48.

46. O'Reilly, C. & Pfeffer, J. (2000). *Hidden Value.* Boston: Harvard Business Press (p. 191).

47. O'Reilly & Pfeffer, 2000, p. 204.

48. Brown, C. & Reich, M. (1989). When does cooperation work? A look at NUMMI and GM Van Nuys. *California Management Review*, 31: 26–37.

49. Henry Mintzberg, one of the most prominent organization and management analysts, distinguishes between types of organizations based on level of standardization of the work. For example, he distinguishes between labor-intensive organizations and knowledge-intensive organizations. Labor-intensive organizations, such as the food and textile industries, are based on standardization of the process (a stereotypical example of this is the production line in an automobile factory in Charlie Chaplin's famous film "Modern Times"), where each employee performs one standard task that is part of the total construction of the product. On the other hand, in knowledge-intensive organizations, which are, in fact, organizations of experts, such as research and development organizations, universities, and so forth, based on the experts' knowledge, – the standardization is of skills. The type of standardization has implications for the variety in the work, the workers' autonomy, decision making processes, the degree of centrality, and so forth. In general, the more the organization is based on standardization of skills, the more decentralized it is. See: Mintzberg, H. (1979). *The Structuring of Organizations: A Synthesis of the Research*. Englewood Cliffs, NJ: Prentice-Hall.

50. O'Reilly & Pfeffer, 2000.

51. O'Reilly & Pfeffer, 2000, pp. 153–5.

52. Chris Argyris and Donald Schon, two well-known writers who have dealt extensively with processes occurring in organizations, distinguish between "stated theory," which consists mainly of declarations, documents, statements by managers, and so forth, and "theory in practice," which can be identified through consistent decisions, behaviors, criteria operating for reward, appreciation, advancement, and so on. One of the arguments of these writers is that there is usually a gap between stated theory and theory in practice, and that in the end people are more influenced by theory in practice, i.e., by actions, examples, behaviors, and decisions, and much less by words and statements. See: Argyris, C. & Schon, D.A. (1996). *Organizational Learning II: Theory, Methods and Practice*. Reading, MA: Addison Wesley.

53. O'Reilly & Pfeffer, 2000, pp. 151–74.

54. The full story of the sausage factory in Johnsonville, which became a "case study" of leadership appears in Ralph Stayer's testimony: Stayer, R. (1993). How I learned to let my workers lead. In G. Wills (ed.) *Your Enterprise School of Management* (pp. 97–113). London: MCB Press.

55. Mintzberg, 1979.

56. Douglas McGregor wrote a classic book in which he distinguishes between "theory X" and "theory Y". Theory X is the assumption that workers are lazy by nature, with all that that implies. Theory Y is the opposite assumption, that people want to express themselves, want to be creative, aim to do their best, and are prepared to work hard. McGregor argues that managers (and

systems) differ from each other in these theories. Management according to theory X is expressed, among other things, by close supervisory mechanisms, and wage policies that emphasize output. On the other hand, management according to theory Y is based more on decentralization, freedom of action, loose supervision, and a considerable degree of trust. See: McGregor, D. (1960). *The Human Side of Enterprise*. New York: McGraw-Hill.

57. Interview with management scholar Tom Peters, taped on video as a case of organizational management. Belasco, J.A. & Stayer, R.C. (1993). Flight of the Buffalo: Soaring to Excellence, Learning to Let Employees Lead. New-York, NY, Warner Books. Stayer R.C. (1990). How I learned to let my workers lead. *Harvard Business Review* November–December, 66–83.

58. Many examples of transformational leadership in organizations appear in the book by Bernard Bass: Bass, B.M. (1985). Leadership and Performance beyond Expectations. New York: Free Press.

59. Popper, M. (1994). *On Managers as Leaders*. Tel Aviv: Ramot Publishers, Tel Aviv University (in Hebrew).

60. The full story of Jaime Escalante appears in a book that presents his educational approach and working methods, as well as follow-up and interviews with his students. Mathews, J. (1988). Escalante: *The Best Teacher in America*. New York: Holt.

61. Eden, D. (1990). *Pygmalion in Management: Productivity as a Self fulfilling Prophecy*. Lexington, MA: Lexington Books.

62. Rosenthal, R. & Jacobson, L. (1968). *Pygmalion in the Classroom*. New York: Holt, Reinhart & Winston.

63. In a leadership development program conducted in Israel for over a decade (since the beginning of the 1990s), with the participation of hundreds of managers from various organizations, they were asked (in the context of the attempt to understand the meaning of the "transformative effect") to mention people who had influenced their lives significantly. An examination of the predominant categories reveals that teachers were most frequently mentioned, followed by parents, with army officers in third place. See: Popper, 1994.

64. Eilon, 1976.

65. Sampson, 1999.

66. Chadha, 1997.

67. Warren Bennis and Burt Nanus examined 90 leaders who were found to be transformational in various organizations. They observed these leaders, studied their working methods and their typical behaviors, and found nothing external common to all of them. Some of the leaders were highly articulate and possessed exceptional oratorical skills, whereas others were totally lacking in such abilities. There were some informal folksy types and some more distant. In a nutshell, the study failed to identify any typical patterns among these leaders. However, one thing they did all have in common was a certain type of thinking, the kind of thinking that is usually described as vision in the American literature on organizations. At the organizational level, vision

includes elements such as a basic philosophy and values that are internalized by the people in the organization, expectations for a certain level of performance, and ethical standards. See: Bennis, W.G. & Nanus, B. (1985). *Leaders: The Strategies for Taking Charge*. New York: Harper & Collins.

68. Mathews, 1988.
69. Cohen, A. (1974). *The Educator Yanush Korchak*. Tel Aviv: Goma Science And Research Books, Tcherikover (in Hebrew).
70. Bass, 1985.
71. Bass, 1985, p. 30.
72. One of the major sources of controversy in the social sciences is the debate between the use of quantitative methodologies – based on figures and conventional statistical tests – and qualitative methodologies, based largely on interviews and participant observation, techniques that are primarily used in anthropological research. It is commonly assumed that qualitative methods enable the researcher to reach a deeper understanding of the phenomenon investigated, whereas their major disadvantage is the lack of ability to generalize to other cases. On the other hand, quantitative methods, based on collecting data from many studies and on standard statistical instruments, permit a greater degree of generalization, whereas their disadvantage is their limited ability to probe into and understand the deeper **processes** underlying the phenomenon investigated, processes that are not measurable. The study described in Bass's book combines both approaches. A discussion on the advantages and disadvantages of each approach with respect to leadership research appears in the following article by Micha Popper: Popper, M. (2002). Salient biases in discussion and research on leadership. In W.K. Parry & R.J.R. Meindl (eds.), *Grounding Leadership Theory and Research: Issues and Perspectives*. Greenwich, CT: Information Age Publishing, pp. 7–19.
73. The first study using factor analysis, and in fact the first questionnaire constructed to discriminate between factors of transformational leadership and the kind known as transactional leadership, was conducted by Bass on a sample of 104 junior army officers, who responded to the questionnaire (known as the MLQ – multifactor leadership questionnaire) with regard to their commanders. In the analysis seven factors with a high (over 1.0) loading coefficient were located, and these accounted for 89.5% of the variance between the 73 items. A description of the construction of the instrument and psychometric data with regard to it appears in Chapter 12 of Bass's book: Bass, B.M. (1985). *Leadership and Performance beyond Expectations*. New York: Free Press (pp. 207–29). Since that questionnaire was developed, it has been used in hundreds of studies, and its validity has been re-examined many times, also in relation to other cultures. The examination of its validity has also been extended to different population groups, to leaders in various spheres in the business and public sector. Today there is a shorter version of the MLQ, consisting of thirty-six items (instead of the seventy-three in the original questionnaire). In addition, the factor "charisma," which appears in the

first questionnaire, is now divided into two factors: "idealized influence" and "inspirational motivation." The development of this instrument in conceptual and psychometric contexts is described in Bass and Avolio's review of the questionnaire in: Bass, B.M. & Avolio, B.J. (1996), *Manual for the Multifactor Leadership Questionnaire*. Palo Alto, CA: Mind Garden.

74. Hollander, E.P. (1978). *Leadership Dynamics*. New York: Free Press.
75. Shamir, B. (1995). Social distance and charisma. Theoretical notes and explanatory study. *Leadership Quarterly*, 1: 19–48.
76. Micha Popper and Ofra Mayseless examined typical behaviors of good parents as reported in the psychological literature on parenting. It emerges that most of the everyday behaviors that characterize good parents also appear in leadership literature as reported by the followers of those leaders who were found to be transformational leaders. Popper, M. & Mayseless, O. (2003). Back to basics: Applying parenting perspective to transformational leadership. *Leadership Quarterly* 14, 41–65.
77. Bass, B.M. (1990). *Bass & Stogdill's Handbook of Leadership: Theory, Research and Management Applications*. New York: Free Press.
78. In the last version of the MLQ, the items that appeared under the heading "intellectual stimulation" were: He (the leader) suggests new ways of performing tasks, causes his people to look at problems from different angles, examines major assumptions to see if they are still relevant, seeks different points of view in solving problems
79. Richard Neustadt, a political scientist from Harvard, examined political leaders' decision making processes. Among others, he studied decisions taken by Franklin Roosevelt. A typical example of the open, informal way in which Roosevelt used to gather input for his decisions and test his assumptions was described by Richard Neustadt and quoted as an example by Henry Mintzberg. See: Mintzberg, H. (1975). The manager's job: Folklore and facts. *Harvard Business Review*, July–August, 53–65.
80. Bass, 1985.
81. Eilon, 1976.
82. Edgar Schein used the expression "basic assumptions" in the psychoanalytical sense, which is taken from the work of psychoanalysts like Wilbur Bion. The fundamental argument is that there is a shared level of collective unconsciousness. This idea finds expression in research on national and organizational cultures. In general, Schein argues that basic assumptions are formed out of the need to create internal integration in order to cope successfully with adaptive processes (e.g., for organizations to succeed in a competitive market). This is the basis for the growth of organizational cultures, which include a language, rituals, and values that dictate their members' typical behaviors. The foundation for such a culture is created mainly during the establishment period of the systems. If the culture enables successful coping, it continues to exist. In other words beneath all the observed behaviors there are basic assumptions. Metaphorically speaking, we can see this as software that

dictates the range of applications that are actually used. See: Schein, E. (1985). *Organizational Culture and Leadership*. San Francisco: Jossey Bass.

83. For a review and analysis of "pessimistic psychology" and positive psychology see the article by Barry Schwartz: Schwartz, B. (2000). Self determination: The tyranny of freedom. *American Psychologist*, January, pp. 79–88. See also the discussion on positive psychology in Argyle's book: Argyle, M. (1987). *The Psychology of Happiness*, New York: Routledge.

84. France de Waal (1996). Good Natured: *The Origins of Right and Wrong in Humans and Other Animals*. Harvard University Press.

85. Experiments and theoretical implications of the simulation known as the "prisoner's dilemma" can be found in: Rapaport, A. & Chammah, A. (1965). *Prisoner's Dilemma*. University of Michigan Press.

86. Shamir, B., House, R.J. & Arthur, M.B. (1993). The motivational effects of charismatic leadership: A self concept based theory. *Organizational Science*, 4: 577–93.

87. Popper, M. (1994). *On Managers as Leaders*. Tel Aviv: Ramot Press, Tel Aviv University.

Chapter 5. The Development of Transformational Leaders

1. Goodwin, D.K. (1995). Franklin Roosevelt 1933–1945. In R.A. Wilson (ed.), *Character Above All: Ten Presidents from FDR to George Bush*. New York: Simon & Schuster (p. 13).

2. Goodwin, ibid., p. 23.

3. Goodwin, p. 16.

4. Several books have been written about Franklin Delano Roosevelt. Two historians (both of them, incidentally, Pulitzer Prize winners) who specialized in Roosevelt's leadership are James McGregor Burns and Doris Goodwin. Their known works on Roosevelt are: Burns, J.M. (1956). *Roosevelt*. New York: Harcourt Brace. Burns, J.M. & Dunn, S. (2001). *The Three Roosevelts: Patrician Leaders who Transformed America*. New York: Atlantic Monthly Press. Goodwin, D.K. (1995). Franklin Roosevelt 1939–1945. In R.A. Wilson (ed.), *Character Above All: Ten Presidents from FDR to George Bush*. New York: Simon and Schuster, pp.13–30.

5. Chadha, Y. (1997). *Gandhi: A Life*. New York: John Wiley & Sons.

6. Sampson, A. (1999). *Mandela*. London: Harper & Collins.

7. Eilon, A. (1976). *Herzl*. Tel Aviv: Am Oved (in Hebrew).

8. Storr, A. (1972). *The Dynamics of Creation*. London: Secker & Warburg.

9. Popper, M. (2001). *Hypnotic Leadership*. Wesport, CT: Praeger.

10. Both Kohut and Winnicott expanded the logic of the dynamics of narcissism – in contexts that are relevant to certain types of leaders. See: Kohut, H. (1971). *The Analysis of the Self*. New York: International University Press. Winnicott, H.P. (1971). *Playing and Reality*. New York: Basic Books. For studies dealing directly with the link between narcissism and leadership: Popper, M.

(1999). The sources of motivation of personalized and socialized charismatic leaders. *Psychoanalysis and Contemporary Thought*, 22, 231–46. Popper, M. (2002). Narcissism and attachment patterns of personalized and socialized charismatic leaders. *Journal of Social and Personal Relations*, 19, 6: 796–808.

11. Freud distinguishes between primary narcissism, which exists in a degree that permits and is perhaps essential to normal development, and secondary narcissism, which is an exaggerated degree and can lead to pathological symptoms. See the discussion on this in: Freud, S. (1986). On narcissism: An introduction. In: A Morrison (ed.), *Essential Papers on Narcissism*. New York: University Press. Pines, M. (1981). Reflections on Mirroring. *International Review of Psychoanalysis*, 11, 27–42.

12. Storr, 1972.

13. House, R.J. & Howell, J.M. (1992). Personality and charismatic leadership. *Leadership Quarterly*, 3, 2: 81–108.

14. On compensation processes in general as they appear in psychoanalytic thinking: Freud, S. (1920). *A General Introduction to Psychoanalysis*. American Edition, Garden City (pp. 363–5). For an analysis based on psychoanalytic concepts in the specific context of compensation processes among leaders, see: Popper, M. (2001).

15. *Diagnostic and Statistical Manual of Mental Disorders* (1994) Fourth edition, American Psychological Association, p. 661.

16. Zaleznik, A. & Kets de Vries, M.F.R. (1975). *Power and the Corporate Mind*. Boston: Houghton Mifflin.

17. Burns, J.M. (1978). *Leadership*. New York: Harper & Row.

18. Freud's theory emphasizes the emotional developmental dynamic mainly in its psychosexual contexts with regard to boys. This, in fact, is one of the criticisms of Freud.

19. Iremonger, L. (1970). *The Fiery Chariot*. London: Secker & Warburg.

20. Elder, G.H. (1974). *Children of the Great Depression*. Chicago: University of Chicago Press.

21. Cox, C.J. & Cooper, C.L. (1989). The making of the British CEO: Childhood, work experience, personality, and management style. *Academy of Management Executive*, 3: 241–5.

22. Eden, D. (1990). *Pygmalion in Management: Productivity as a Self-fulfilling Prophecy*. Lexington, MA: Lexington.

23. Steinberg, B.S. (2001). The making of female presidents and prime ministers. The impact of birth order, sex of siblings and father-daughter dynamics. *Political Psychology*, 22: 89–114. Raz, G. (2001). Socialization for leadership. Doctoral dissertation (in preparation). Haifa: Department of Psychology. University of Haifa.

24. Pinner, F. (1965). Parental observation and political distrust. *Annals of the American Academy of Political and Social Science*, vol. 361, September: 58–70.

25. Wilkinson, R. (1964). *Gentlemanly Power: British Leadership and the Public School Tradition.* London: Oxford University Press.
26. Matthews, J. (1988). Escalante: *The Best Teacher in America.* New York: Holt.
27. Lindholm, C. (1990). *Charisma.* London: Blackwell.
28. Emmons, R. (1985). *Manson in his Own Words.* New York: Grove Press (p. 183).
29. Bromberg, N. & Small, V. (1984). *Hitler's Psychopathology.* New York: International University Press.
30. Bernard Bass composed a kind of "encyclopedia" of the various psychological studies conducted in the field of leadership. Some of these studies examined the link between self confidence and (positive) leadership. Bass referred to this in his book of 1985 (Chapters 4 and 5). Mowday (1979), in a study conducted among sixty-five school principals concerning their treatment of four hard decisions, found that those who had a lot of self confidence were perceived more as leaders, as more convincing. Kipnis and Lane (1962) found that self confidence was a discriminating variable between principals perceived as leaders and those not perceived as leaders. Those with self confidence made much use of interpersonal communication, rewards, and promises, as opposed to principals lacking self confidence, who used more coercion and formal rules. Similar findings were reported by Kaplan (1986). See: Mowday, R.T. (1979). Leader characteristics, self-confidence, and methods of upward influence in organizational decision situations. *Academy of Management Journal*, 22: 709–25. Kaplan, R.E. (1986). The warp and woof of the general manager's job. In B. Eider & D. Schoorman (eds.), *Facilitating Work Effectiveness.* Lexington, MA: Lexington Books. Kipnis, D. & Lane, W.P. (1962). Self-confidence and leadership. *Journal of Applied Psychology*, 46: 291–5. Bass, B.M. (1985). Leadership and Performance beyond Expectations. New York: Free Press.
31. McCullough, D. (1995). Harry Truman 1945–1953. In R.A. Wilson (1995). *Character Above All.* New York: Simon & Schuster (pp. 39–59).
32. McCullough, 1995.
33. Sampson, 1999.
34. Eilon, 1976.
35. Bar-Zohar, M. (1968). *Ben-Gurion: the Armed Prophet.* Englewood Cliffs, NJ: Prentice-Hall. Teveth, S. (1985). *Ben-Gurion and the Palestinian Arabs. From Peace to War.* Oxford, New York: Oxford University Press.
36. Goodwin, 1995.
37. An initial attempt to study genetic aspects of leadership was presented by: Johnson, A.M., Vernon, P.A., Molson, M., & (1998). *Born to Lead: A Behavior Genetic Investigation of Leadership Ability.* Paper presented at a national meeting of the Society for Industrial Organizational Psychology, Dallas, TX.
38. The major "classic" theories relating to the critical developmental importance of the period of infancy and early childhood are those of Sigmund Freud and John Bowlby: Freud, S. (1920). *A General Introduction to Psychoanalysis.*

Garden City, American Edition (pp. 363–5). Bowlby, J. (1969). *Attachment and Loss: Vol. 1, Attachment*. New York: Basic Books.

39. Eilon, 1976, p. 27.
40. Eilon, 1976, p. 29.
41. Popper, M. (2000). The development of charismatic leaders. *Political Psychology*, 21: 729–44.
42. Chadha, 1997, p. 43.
43. Burns, 1956.
44. Sampson, 1999.
45. Bowlby, J. (1969). *Attachment and Loss: Vol. 1 Attachment*. New York: Basic Books. Bowlby, J. (1973). *Attachment and Loss: Vol. 2. Separation*. New York: Basic Books.
46. Darwin, C. (1958). *The Autobiography and Selected Letters*. New York: Dover. Lorenz, K. (1966). Evolution and Modification of Behavior. London: Methuen.
47. Lorenz, 1966.
48. Cairns, R.B. & Johnson, D.L. (1965). The development of interspecies social attachment. *Psychonomic Science*, 2: 337–8.
49. Harlow, H.F. & Harlow, M.K. (1965). The affectional systems. In A.M. Schrier, H.F. Harlow & F. Stolwitz (eds.), *Behavior of Nonhuman Primates*, vol. 2. New York: Academic Press.
50. Ainsworth, M.D.S., Blehar, M., Wates, E. & Wall, S. (1978). *Patterns of Attachment: A Psychological Study of Strange Situations*. Hillsdale, NJ: Earlbaum.
51. Ainsworth et al., 1978.
52. A comprehensive survey of the research on attachment was presented by Cassidy: Cassidy, J. (1999). The nature of the child's ties. In J. Cassidy & P.R. Shaver (eds.), *Handbook of Attachment: Theory, Research and Clinical Implications* (pp. 3–20). New York: Guilford Press.
53. Hazan, C. & Shaver, P. (1987). Romantic love conceptualized as an attachment process. *Journal of Personality and Social Psychology*, 52: 511–24.
54. Mayseless, O., Sharabany, R. & Sagi, A. (1997). Attachment concerns of others as manifested in parental, spousal and friendship relationships. *Personal Relationships*, 4: 255–69.
55. Popper, M. & Mayseless, O. (2002). Internal world of transformational leaders. In B. Avolio & F. Yammarino (eds.), *Transformational/Charismatic Leadership: The Road Ahead*. New York: Elsevier Science Publications, pp. 203–30.
56. Berne, E. (1972). *Games People Play*. Harmondsworth, MDDX: Penguin Books.
57. For a discussion of theoretical and empirical links between attachment, namely internal working models formed in early childhood, and manifestations of transformational behavior, see the following articles: Popper, M., Mayseless, O., & Castelnovo, O. (2000). Transformational leadership and attachment. *Leadership Quarterly*, 11: 267–289. Popper, M. & Mayseless, O. (2003).

Back to basics: Applying parenting perspective to transformational leadership. *Leadership Quarterly*, 14, 41–65.

58. Popper, M., Mayseless, O., & Castelnovo, O. (2000). *Leadership Quarterly*, 11, 267–89. Mikulincer, M. & Florian, V. (1995). Appraisal of and coping with a real-life stressful situation: The contribution of attachment styles. *Journal of Personality and Social Psychology*, 21: 406–14.

59. Plomin, R., Scheier, M.F., Bergeman, C.S., Pederson, N.L., Nesserlroade, J. & McClearn, G. (1992). Optimism, pessimism and mental health: A twin adoption analysis. *Personality and Individual Differences*, 13: 921–30.

60. Zuckerman, M. (2001). Optimism and pessimism. Biological foundations. In E.C. Chang (ed.), *Optimism and Pessimism: Implications for Theory, Research and Practice*. Washington, DC: American Psychological Association (pp. 169–88). Hjelle, L.A., Busch, E.A. & Warren, J.E. (1996). Explanatory style, dispositional optimism, and reported parental behavior. *Journal of Genetic Psychology*, 157: 489–499.

61. Chadha, 1997. Gandhi, M. (1957). *An Autobiography: The Story of My Experiments with the Truth*. Boston: Beacon Press.

62. Chadha, 1997, p. 45.

63. Chadha, 1997, p. 63.

64. Sampson, 1999, p. 523.

65. Sampson, 1999, p. 523.

66. Kanungo, R.N. & Mendonca, M. (1996). *Ethical Dimensions in Leadership*. Beverley Hills, CA: Sage.

67. Zahn-Waxler, C., Schiro, K., Robinson, J.L., Emde, R.N. & Schmitz, S. (2001). Empathy and pro-social patterns in young MZ and DZ twins. Development and genetic and environmental influences. In R.N. Emde & J.K. Hewitt (eds.), *Infancy to Early Childhood: Genetic and Environmental influences on Developmental Change*. New York, NY: Oxford University Press (pp. 141–62).

68. Grusec, J.E. & Dix, T. (1986). The socialization of prosocial behavior: Theory and reality. In C. Zahn-Waxler, E.M. Cummings, & R. Iannotti (eds.), *Altruism and Aggression, Biological and Social Origins*. Cambridge: Cambridge University Press (pp. 218–27).

69. Burns, 1978.

70. Avolio, B.J. & Gibbons, T.C. (1988). Developing transformational leaders: A life span approach. In J.A. Conger & R.N. Kanungo (eds.), *Charismatic Leadership: The Elusive Factor in Organizational Effectiveness*. San Francisco: Jossey-Bass (pp. 276–308).

71. Popper, M. & Mayseless, O. (2002). *The Building Blocks of Leadership Development: A Psychological Conceptual Framework*. Haifa, Dept. of Psychology, University of Haifa).

72. Bandura, A. (ed.) (1995). *Self-efficacy in Changing Societies*. New York, NY: Cambridge University Press.

73. Sampson, 1999.

74. Burns, 1978.
75. Sampson, 1999, p. 10.
76. Sampson, 1999, p. 10.
77. Sampson, 1999, p. 10.
78. Sampson, 1999, p. 11.
79. Chadha, 1997.
80. Chadha, 1997, p. 104.
81. Chadha, 1997, p. 191.
82. Kotter, J. (1990). *A Force for Change: How Leadership Differs from Management*. New York: The Free Press.
83. Akin, G. (1987). Varieties of managerial learning. *Organizational Dynamics*, 16, 2: 36–48.
84. Bandura, 1995.
85. Bandura, A. (1977). Self-efficacy: Toward a unifying theory of behavioral change. *Psychological Review*, 84: 191–215.
86. Chadha, 1997.
87. Bennis, W.G. (1989). *On Becoming a Leader*. New York: Addison Wesley. Zakay, E. & Scheinfeld, A. (1993). *Outstanding Battalion Commanders*. Research Report, School of Leadership Development, Israel Defense Forces (IDF) (in Hebrew).
88. Popper, M. (2001). *Hypnotic Leadership: Leaders, Followers and the Loss of Self*. Westport, CT: Praeger.
89. Bennis, W.G. & Nanus, B. (1985). *Leaders: The Strategies for Taking Charge*. New York: Harper & Collins. Bennis, W.G. (1989). *On Becoming a Leader*. New York: Addison Wesley.
90. Ainsworth et al., 1978.
91. Skinner, B.F. (1989). *Recent Issues in the Analysis of Behavior*. Columbus, Ohio: Merril Pub. Co.
92. Bandura, A. (1977). *Social Learning Theory*. New Jersey, Englewood Cliffs.
93. Bandura, A., Ross, D. & Ross, S. (1963). Imitation of film-mediated aggressive models. *Journal of Abnormal and Social Psychology*, 66: 3–11.
94. Avolio, B. (1999). F*ull Leadership Development*. London: Sage Publications.
95. Johnson, A.M., Vernon, P.A., Molson, M., Harris, J.A. & Jang, K.L. (1998). *Born to Lead: A Behavior Genetic Investigation of Leadership Ability*. Paper presented at the national meeting of the Society for Industrial Organizational Psychology, Dallas, TX.

Chapter 6. Conclusion

1. A critique of the history of some of the major ideas and theories in human thought appears in the following book: Gellner, E. (1985). The Psychoanalytic Movement. The Cunning of the Unreason. London: Fontana Press.
2. Bass, B.M. (1990). *Bass & Stogdill's Handbook of Leadership: Theory, Research and Management Applications*. New York: Free Press.

3. Bass, 1990.
4. Heifetz, R.H. (1994). *Leadership Without Easy Answers*. Cambridge, Mass: Harvard University.
5. Reeves, R. (1995). John F. Kennedy. In R.A. Wilson (ed.), *Character Above All*. New York: Simon & Schuster (pp. 82–104).
6. Reeves, 1995.
7. Leadership: Lessons from Mount Rushmore. An interview with James McGregor Burns by James Bailey and Ruth Axelrod. *Leadership Quarterly*, 2002, p. 17.
8. Burns, J.M. (1956). *Roosevelt*. New York: Harcourt Brace.
9. Reeves, 1995.
10. Hegel, G.W.F. (1981). *The Berlin Phenomenology*. Edited and translated by M.J. Perty. Dordrocht, Boston: D. Reisdel.
11. Adam Smith (1937). *The Wealth of Nations*. New York: Random House.
12. Shenhav, Y. (1995). *The Organization Machine*. Tel Aviv: Schocken Press (in Hebrew). See also Harr, J.E. & Johnson, J. (1988). *The Rockefeller Century*. New York: Scribner.
13. Burns, J.M. & Dun, S. (2001). *The Three Roosevelts. Patrician Leaders who Transformed America*. New York: Atlantic Monthly Press.
14. Ronen, A. (1992). Leadership in philosophical thought. In M. Popper & A. Ronen, *On Leadership*. Tel Aviv: Defense Ministry Publications (in Hebrew) pp. 13–41.
15. Lipshitz, R. (1991). "Either a medal or corporal." The effects of success and failure on the evaluation of decision making and decision makers. *Organizational Behavior and Human Decision Processes*, 44: 380–435.
16. Adigas, Y. (1979). *Flawed Leadership: Causes and Treatment*. Tel Aviv: Cherikover Press (in Hebrew). Fiedler, F.F. (1967). *A Theory of Leadership Effectiveness*. New York: McGraw Hill.
17. A comprehensive analysis of this argument is presented in: Burns, J.M. (1978). *Leadership*. New York: Harper & Row.
18. Schwartz, B. (2000). *Abraham Lincoln. Forge of National Memory*. Chicago: University of Chicago Press.
19. O'Reilly, C.A. & Pfeffer, J. (2000). *Hidden Value*. Boston, MA: Harvard Business School.
20. Bass, B.M. (1985). *Leadership and Performance beyond Expectations*. New York: Free Press.
21. Peters, T. & Waterman, R.H. (1982). *In Search of Excellence*. New York: Warner Books. O'Reilly & Pfeffer, 2000.
22. Edgar Schein dealt with the study of the sources of "cultures of organizations" and found that there is great weight to values that were imprinted by the founding fathers on organizations. His arguments are presented in the book: Schein, E. (1985). *Organizational Culture and Leadership*. San Francisco: Jossey Bass.

23. Schwartz, B. (2000). Self-determination: The tyranny of freedom. *American Psychologist*, January: 79–88.

24. Klerman, G.L., Lavori, P.W., Rice, J., et al. (1985). Birth control trends in rates of major depressive disorder among relatives of patients with affective disorders. *Archives of General Psychiatry*, 42: 689–93.

25. Kouzes, J.M. & Posner, B.J. (1987). *The Leadership Challenge*. San Francisco: Jossey-Bass.

26. Vardi, Y., Wiener, Y. & Popper, M. (1989). The value content of organizational mission as a factor of the commitment of members. *Psychological Reports*, 65, 27–34.

27. Bennis, W.G. & Nanus, B. (1985). *Leaders: The Strategies for Taking Charge*. New York: Harper and Collins.

28. Peters & Waterman, 1982.

29. Sampson, A. (1999). *Mandela*. London: Harper and Collins (p. 113).

Index

About the Author

MICHA POPPER is Co-Director of the Center for Outstanding Leadership and a Senior Lecturer in the Department of Psychology at the University of Haifa. He is also former Commanding Officer of the School for Leadership Development of the Israeli Defense Forces. He is author of *Hypnotic Leadership: Leaders, Followers and the Loss of Self* (Praeger, 2001).